ROMAN IDEAS OF DEITY

ROMAN IDEAS OF DEITY

IN THE LAST CENTURY BEFORE THE CHRISTIAN ERA

LECTURES DELIVERED IN OXFORD FOR THE
COMMON UNIVERSITY FUND

BY

W. WARDE FOWLER, M.A.

HON. LL.D. EDINBURGH, HON. D.LITT. MANCHESTER
AUTHOR OF
'ROMAN FESTIVALS OF THE REPUBLIC,'
'SOCIAL LIFE IN ROME IN THE AGE OF CICERO
'RELIGIOUS EXPERIENCE OF THE ROMAN PEOPLE ETC.

WIPF & STOCK · Eugene, Oregon

Wipf and Stock Publishers
199 W 8th Ave, Suite 3
Eugene, OR 97401

Roman Ideas of Deity
In the Last Century Before the Christian Ere
By Fowler, W. Warde
ISBN 13: 978-1-60608-307-9
Publication date 9/24/2010
Previously published by Macmillan, 1914

CONTENTS

LECTURE I

SKETCH OF THE COURSE: DOMESTIC DEITIES

Roman and Italian religion of last century B.C. usually neglected by students of the threshold of Christianity. Cicero's *de Nat. Deorum*, its value and shortcomings. Cicero's ideas of the supernatural in the last two years of his life. His view of "superstitio." Did he mean, like Lucretius, to eradicate it ? The Italian's difficulty in realising divinity. Four ways in which he realised it in last century B.C. : the first, domestic deity, subject of the rest of this lecture. Vesta and Penates, survivals of animism, act as antidotes to exotic polytheism. Genius, akin to the idea of *numen*, and on the way to divinity. Was it mortal ? In Cicero's time a *deus mortalis* : later modification of this. Later developments of Genius, and their meaning in two later periods. Leading idea, divine permanence of thing or institution. Cult of the dead : makes no real contribution to the idea of deity .   1

LECTURE II

JUPITER AND THE TENDENCY TO MONOTHEISM

Decay of the old Italian *numina* : also of the gods of Rome, anthropomorphised under Greek influence. One exception, Jupiter (*Optimus Maximus*), deity of heaven, good faith, and oaths, and protector of the empire. Monotheistic background in animistic religions. Illustrations from China, Borneo, etc. The Latin Jupiter of the *feriae Latinae* may represent this background in Italy. Evidence in the Flamen Dialis, and the oath of the Fetiales. Moral power of Jupiter best seen in oaths, taken in the open air, the all-seeing Heaven-god being witness. Power of the oath at Rome. Idea of a supreme Deity in last century B.C. : evidence of Lucretius, Cicero, Varro. Two reasons why Jupiter Capitolinus could be identified with the Stoic supreme Deity   29

LECTURE III

COSMIC IDEAS OF DEITY

Sun-worship not universal, and why. No distinct trace of it in Italy in early times. New interest in the sun in Cicero's time : due to Posidonius. Sun *dux et princeps* of the heavenly bodies. Traces of sun-worship in the Augustan Age. Prominence of Fortuna in last century B.C. What is meant by Fortuna: was she a deity ? Origin of Fortuna as a deity of Latium, concerned with fortune-telling but not with blind chance, which was never congenial to the Roman mind. Meaning of Τύχη in Panaetius : in Polybius, where the word sometimes means a natural process of evolution. Fortuna in Cicero is clearly chance, or the incalculable in human life : this the result of the uncertainty of life in that age. Fortuna in Lucretius seems to mean Natura. Fortuna in Caesar is simply chance or accident : but in Sallust, etc. a capricious power, unexplained. In Virgil Fortuna is in some degree a moral force. Fortuna on the border of deus-land : does she cross it under the Empire ? 55

LECTURE IV

THE RISE OF THE IDEA OF THE MAN-GOD

Roman religion, human and social, as treated by Cicero and Varro, who look on religion as a State-made institution. When this religion breaks down, a substitute can be found in the worship of rulers. Tendency in this direction in last century B.C. : the divine element in Man, illustrated from literature of this period. But the true Roman religion traditionally discouraged such a tendency, not recognising demi-gods, descent from gods, or divinity of rulers. Hence the caution needed in introducing the Man-god, and the failure of Antony's attempts. Success came from Greece and East : sketch of rise of the Man-god in Egypt and Greece. What reality could there be in such an idea at Rome ? 81

LECTURE V

THE DEIFICATION OF CAESAR

Distinction between official and popular deification: the latter chiefly of interest here. Need for a "Sôter" in Rome. Julius hardly so looked on in his lifetime. Precedents for cult of Man in Roman history. Cult of Julius official and little noticed by contemporaries, except in East, *e.g.* Ephesus : discouraged by

CONTENTS

himself. After Munda, statue in temple of Quirinus: after January 1, 44, serious attempts of Antony, not to be made too much of. But after the murder this cult seems to become popular: excitement and despair. Importance of January 1, 42. Policy of Augustus in regard to cult: no official cult allowed: use of Genius: no place for Man-god in *ius sacrum*. *Per contra*: evidence from poets: who look on Augustus as potentially *deus*, and once or twice anticipate his apotheosis proleptically. The cult in the Latin provinces: Genius or Numen Augusti, in connection with Dea Roma 107

LECTURE VI

DEGRADATION OF THE IDEA OF DEITY IN THE AUGUSTAN AGE

The Olympian gods arrived at Rome in their least inspiring form. They were not elevated by noble sculpture. Apollo a good example: killed by poetry in Augustan age, being used as a symbol only. Saved from extinction only by association with sun-worship. Mars degraded as symbol of war: survives as a poetical figure. Vesta escaped both symbolism and mythology. Survey of the Augustan poets in relation to Deity: Virgil's real love was for the *di agrestes*; the Olympians only useful as machinery. So too Tibullus, though he has a liking for mystery religions. Horace's changing attitude to religion: his gods on the whole lifeless. Propertius quite cold, and also Ovid: their gods have no life 134

SUMMARY OF THE RESULTS OF THE INVESTIGATION . . . 158

INDEX 163

LECTURE I

SKETCH OF THE COURSE: DOMESTIC DEITIES

MY object in these few lectures is to gain some idea of what the Roman and Italian, learned or unlearned, thought about deity and the divine nature in the age immediately preceding the Christian era. The tendency to-day is to concentrate attention on the Hellenistic age, and on the whole range of mystical Graeco-Egyptian literature which was the natural result of the ideas of that age; or again on the types of oriental religion which obtained a footing, more or less secure, in the Roman world of the Empire. No doubt such studies are more profitable than any that Rome and Italy can supply. On the other hand, the Italian side of the great religious problem of this age has never, I think, been systematically treated on its own merits. I know of no one who has been through the voluminous Latin literature of that time with the special object of ascertaining, if possible, what ideas of divine power were current in Italy, apart from those of Greek philosophers. Even the very instructive edition of Cicero's work on the nature of the gods, by the veteran scholar, Dr. Joseph B. Mayor, does not exactly answer my purpose; for both introductions and commentary are of necessity mainly occupied with the Greek originals used by Cicero, and all such matter as may throw light on them.

My original plan, it is true, was to use these three books of Cicero as the basis of my lectures. I read them again, as I had often read them before, looking for something to my purpose without finding much. I am well aware of their great value in certain ways, and especially in the presentation, in the second book, of Stoic ideas of religion as held by the Syrian Posidonius, a man who seems during the last few years to have reappeared in the world, and to be made responsible not only for the Stoicism of the next age, but for astrology by M. Cumont, for the sixth *Aeneid* by Norden, for mysticism by Wendland, as well as for the history and geography of the age, through Diodorus and Strabo.[1] In estimating the mental treasures of this extraordinary man, Cicero is in this work and others of the same time undoubtedly of great value. But this was not what I proposed to myself.

And to say the truth the *de Natura Deorum* is by no means wholly satisfying. The subject is one of enormous difficulty, far beyond Cicero's mental reach. We have only to think of the extreme difficulty

---

[1] Cumont, *Astrology and Religion*, p. 83 foll. Norden, *Virgil, Aen. VI.* p. 20 foll. Wendland, *Die hellenistisch-römische Kultur* (1912), p. 134 foll. Schmekel, *Die mittlere Stoa*, p. 85 foll. Mr. Bevan, in *Stoics and Sceptics*, p. 98 foll., has some very useful remarks on Posidonius. To " make men at home in the universe " was, he aptly says, the real mission of this encyclopaedist.

of fixing the idea of the supernatural at any historical period, to see that a man of the world like Cicero, however gifted, could hardly be qualified for such work.

For that idea is the result of a number of different currents of tradition and reflection, of the intermixture of races and systems of education, of social habits and the beliefs that they have engendered. Amateur's work will not find a path through subject-matter like this, and Cicero may fairly be described as an interested amateur. Amateur we must call him, though he wrote, according to his habit, on the foundation of the works of others who can perhaps hardly be called by that name, save in so far as it is applicable to all the philosophers of that age. Varro, the fragments of whose writings are often of great value for our subject, was probably less of an amateur: he had a wider knowledge and a harder head. Lucretius is less so than either, for he was not a busy public man like the other two, but a real student and in deadly earnest. But Cicero was an amateur not only because he did not think much for himself, but because he did not really believe his subject to be of vital interest to humanity. Meditation on the nature of God did not come to him as a necessity: it came because he was intellectually interested in all such questions.

Yet in spite of Cicero's amateurishness, we must not forget that the *de Natura Deorum*, like all his strictly philosophical works, was written at the close of his life, when he was much moved by an accumulation of trials and troubles, political and domestic. These culminated in the loss of his daughter, and this last blow put him in a mental condition so emotional as almost to make a mystic of him for a time.[1] Tullia died early in 45 B.C., and Cicero still had two and a half years of life before him. In these years, as a man of sorrows trying to console himself with philosophy, all his philosophical works were written; the *Academica*, the *Tusculans*, the *de Finibus*, the *de Officiis*, and the *de Natura Deorum*,[2] this last followed by the *de Divinatione* and *de Fato*, subjects closely connected with it. Death, future life, prophecy, duty, deity—subjects like these were now in the mind of this quick and sensitive man. I do not think it has been sufficiently noticed that these writings point to an era in his life in which he was really bringing his mind to bear on great questions of human interest, as he had never yet done, except perhaps when, as a younger man by ten years, he wrote the *de Republica* and the *Somnium Scipionis*,—in another period of recovery from serious misfortune and depression.

So in spite of his habitual dilettantism, I cannot but think that the three books on the nature of Deity were the work of one in some sense seeking after God. If he had been living in one of the great oriental cities, he might well have been one

---

[1] *The Religious Experience of the Roman People*, p. 385 foll.
[2] See Mayor's *de Natura Deorum*, vol. iii. p. xxv.

of the "God-fearers" (σεβόμενοι), of whom Professor Lake has had much to say in his book on the earlier epistles of St. Paul:[1] men, that is, interested in the worship of the Jews or some other oriental people, such as the centurion who built the Jews a synagogue, or the Roman soldier Cornelius of Acts x.[2] Such men would join in the worship of the synagogue without actually submitting to become proselytes : men who mark the spirit of the age, in that they have given up the religion of the old City-state as no longer really religion, and are disposed to satisfy their yearnings of heart by taking lessons from other peoples in religion, either intellectually or emotionally, or both. But I am merely fancying for a moment what might have happened had Cicero been what he was not; in reality he was a Roman man of the world, living in Italy, and he never got as far as this. He was indeed the last-born son of the old City-state, and he never, in principle at least, gave up its worship. If you had asked him whether he believed in the existence of the divine inhabitants of the city, I think he would have answered "Yes" without hesitation, but with a mental reservation for all except perhaps Jupiter and Vesta. If you asked him the same question about the deities of the household and the spirits of the dead, I believe he would have answered in the affirmative with little reserva-

---

[1] Lake, *Earlier Epistles of St. Paul*, p. 37 foll.

[2] Cp. also Acts xvii. 10 foll. Professor Lake, on p. 65, defines the God-fearers as men who were dissatisfied with their own position, and were easily capable of becoming fervent believers.

tion. The presiding deities of the household were a part of his mental furniture, as definitely fixed in his mind as the trees growing round the ancestral farm at Arpinum; while the great protecting deity of Rome, and the spirit of the everlasting hearth-fire of the city, were simply a part of his life as an active Roman citizen. But beyond this I should not like to attempt to fathom his religious consciousness.

So much for the personal aspect of the *de Natura Deorum*. Now let us look at it for a moment in the light of the thinking power and the religious tendencies of the period. How far does it really represent an actual current either of thought or feeling? How far is it rooted in the life of Rome and Italy?

Not long ago Professor J. S. Reid read an excellent paper to our Oxford Philological Society on Cicero's philosophical works, and his genuine admiration was delightful and stimulating. But he did not mention the one serious defect even of these last works of Cicero's life: a defect which we should probably also find, were they extant in abundance, in the Greek writers whom Cicero followed, Posidonius, Antiochus, Philodemus, and the rest,—that their thinking was not rooted in the life of the world around them. So far as we can guess, these writers only modified old systems of philosophy to suit their own age: they did not grow naturally and organically out of the soil, as did the old Socratic school. But if philosophy is to be fertile, it must not detach itself from life. "Its office," said Dr. Caird, " is to bring life to clear self-consciousness, as the old Greek philosophy did."¹ I think this exactly suggests the weak point of Cicero, what makes him fall flat to the ordinary reader, if not to a student like Professor Reid. The *Tusculans* for example, and the *de Officiis*, were wholesome and readable, but they have never really roused mankind. They suggest that Panaetius and the others may have been also out of touch with real life, and have gained their Roman reputation rather from their novelty— I mean the novelty of their thoughts for a Roman— than from the living force which mirrors human life. Almost the same may be said of Seneca, and this is, I think, the right way to explain the obvious gulf between his life and his philosophy. Neither with Cicero nor Seneca does philosophy seem to come straight from the only fountain-head of real thought in ethics and religion—the problems of the life around you. The last enthusiast about Cicero, Zielinski, in his book *Cicero im Wandel der Jahrhunderte*, seems to miss this point entirely.²

If this is so in Cicero's philosophy generally, it is even more so in what we may call his theological writings. The world had long ago entered on an age of theological thought, in succession to an age of simple and almost unconscious religious practice. If theology is religion brought to self-consciousness,³ this was an age of theology; for the old religious rites, and their meaning and object, had all become

---
[1] Caird, *The Evolution of Religion in the Greek Philosophies*, ch. ii.
[2] See his account of Cicero's ethic, p. 70 foll. (ed. 2, 1908).
[3] Caird, *op. cit.* vol. i. p. 31.

matter of questioning. Yet Cicero's theology does not really tackle the great problem of Italian religious life—What is the meaning and object of these rites, and to what kind of beings are they really addressed ? What can we know of the powers whom we thus worship ? Cicero speculates in the modes of thought of his masters and models—he rarely or never, like Lucretius or even Virgil, faces the facts right in front of him. Once only, as we shall see in a moment, does he seem to inherit the earnest spirit of Lucretius —the scorn without the remedy.

If the religion in question, *i.e.* that of Rome and Italy, had been at this time a genuine product, full of life, this theology might have been of real and permanent interest. It would have found a rich soil to grow in. But we must do Cicero the justice to say that in Rome, and very largely in Italy too, there was little life left in the religious forms and conceptions. Lucretius utterly despised them, and so also did Cicero at times, though they used different terms, Cicero calling it all *superstitio*, Lucretius *religio*.[1] This is not indeed generally recognised as regards Cicero, but whoever will read the first few pages of Mayor's introduction to his third volume of the *Natura Deorum* will find strong grounds for this view. Or listen to a passage quoted by him from the second book, *de Divinatione* (sec. 148): "To say the truth, *superstitio* has spread among all peoples,

---

[1] For these two difficult terms, see Mayor's note on *de Natura Deorum*, ii. 72 (vol. ii. p. 183); and W. Otto, *Archiv für Religionswissenschaft*, vol. xii. (1909), p. 533 foll.

SKETCH OF THE COURSE

has captured almost every mind, taking advantage of human weakness. It is ever pursuing and driving you, turn in which direction you will, whether you listen to a prophet or an omen, whether you sacrifice a victim or catch sight of a bird of warning, whether you meet an eastern soothsayer or an Italian haruspex, whether you see lightning or hear thunder, or find some object struck." He adds that sleep, which should be a refuge from these terrors, itself, in dreams, produces anxiety and fear. This is Lucretius in prose, neither more nor less. At the very end of his life, with his emotions tending to mysticism, Cicero says plainly thus in his own person, *i.e.* in argument against his brother Quintus, that the religion of the individual is really *superstitio, Aberglaube*. Of the State he could not possibly say that, though as a matter of fact the practical religion of the State was not very different; nor could he say it of the family. But it is certainly possible that when he wrote this *de Divinatione*, which followed the *de Natura Deorum* after a short interval, he had come nearer to the Lucretian point of view, reaching it, however, quite as much through Stoicism as Epicurism. Such a conclusion would be perfectly natural in a man who had at last begun to face these questions, and who saw the Republic, the sole *raison d'être* of state religion, falling before his eyes.

Dr. Mayor contends that Cicero's object even in the earlier of the two works was to eradicate this *superstitio* from the minds of men, and to show the value of a rational religion; and that he combines with this the speculative aim of expounding to his countrymen the theological views of the leading Greek philosophers. I cannot tell what Cicero might have achieved if he had lived a while longer, and given up his time to a more scientific study of his subject, as Lucretius had done. But on the whole I doubt whether under any circumstances he would have taken on himself the office of missionary. If he had been tending in that direction we should have found, in these later works of his, greater independence, more fervour of exposition, more of the spirit of Lucretius. I doubt if Cicero was equal to putting inspiration into a theology; to the last he remained more or less critical, true in the main to the principles of the academic school. Far less was it possible for him to get back from theology to religion. The real value of his work is in giving us the best speculative ideas of deity current in his time; and Dr. Mayor is no doubt right in calling his second book *Natura Deorum*, on the Stoic doctrines, one of the most important contributions to theological thought that has come down to us from classical antiquity.

But I do not propose in these lectures to expound Cicero's exposition of the expositions of his predecessors. I want to get at the notions of divinity held by the ordinary Roman, and I shall only use Cicero as a help here and there. The philosophers as such I may leave aside : I am not specially concerned with any of their systems, save in so far as they affected the educated Roman of this age. So far as they affected him in regard to the idea of God, they did so through pre-existing Roman modes of thought—if we can apply the word "thought" to these traditional inheritances—and through other tendencies which had for some time been growing in force.

And here I must say once for all that in my view the conception of divinity, as distinct from mere supernaturalism, was for a Roman or Italian peculiarly difficult. His interest was centred in the cult rather than in the objects of it; a tendency against which it was the mission of the Jewish prophets unceasingly to contend, as destructive in the long run of the noblest ideas of God and his relation to his people. He did not speculate on the nature of his *numina*, or invent stories about them; the priests and the cults were there to keep him in right relation with these manifestations of the Power controlling his life and welfare, and there was an end of his interest in it. It did not occur to him, as to Greek thinkers in the age of enlightenment, to try and pass beyond the manifestations to the Power behind them. When the Greek anthropomorphic deities were imported to Rome, his mental attitude to them, so far as we can guess, was naturally much the same; he liked to see the cult, and feel that it was being properly carried out, just as Horace, wandering about the Forum and Circus, took it into his head to look in at evening service ("adsistere divinis," *Sat.* i. 114); but he failed to realise divinity in the Beings to whom such rites were paid, whether Italian or Greek. Thus it was not natural to the Roman to meditate on the idea of God; and the only advantage he had over the Greek in his notion of divinity was that he did not, until the Greeks taught him to do so, associate it with absurdity or immorality, only with force and activity, which might be brought by due propitiation into the service of man.

There were, however, at least four ways in which, by conviction and practice, the Romans and Italians of that age seem to have dimly realised the idea of deity. The first of these was in the worship of the family, which continued to express in some degree the inheritance of a traditional animism, passing at one or two points into something near akin to what we call divinity. The second was in the worship not of the family but of the State; a tendency, probably the result in part of an inherited strain of monotheism, to look on the great deity of the heaven, also the protecting deity of the State and the Empire, yet a *numen* of the ancient kind, seated on the Capitoline hill, as essentially the same as the world-spirit of the philosophers from Plato to Posidonius, now becoming familiar to the educated at Rome. Thirdly, there was a growing habit among all strata of society in that age, so full of uncertainty for human life and property, to look away from the old ideas of protecting power, whether of family or State, to lose faith in all steadying influences, and to recognise and eventually to adore, a principle (if such a word may be used of it) of blind chance or irresistible fate, linking on the idea, in some at least of its aspects, with an old Roman cult of a deity Fortuna, with which in reality it had little or nothing to do. Fourthly, and eventually most universal of all, there was the tendency, found throughout the eastern half of the Empire for long past, to apply to men of great position, talent, or benevolence, the outward forms of religion, as though they were indeed themselves deities, and gradually to elevate them more and more distinctly into the place once held, as helpers and protectors, by the old State gods, regarding them with faith and hope as saviours of society.

These four ways of recognising and realising the idea of deity will form the subjects of my first five lectures; two of which will be devoted to the last of the four, because it eventually became the most striking part of the State religion of the whole Roman Empire. Three at least of the four, as you will have noticed, are characteristic of Man in society, in social groups; but the third, the belief in Fortuna, belongs rather to the individual, as victim of the caprice of luck or the decrees of fate, until it later became incorporated with the State religion of Caesar-worship. But the individual could not find permanent satisfaction in Fortuna, which could arouse in him no real religious emotion. The time was, however, at hand when he was to find this satisfaction, the comfort and confidence of a conscience sensible of sin and hopeless of a life beyond this one, in the mystery religions of Eastern origin, the cults of Isis, Cybele, Mithras, and finally in the Pauline conception of Christianity. But in the period I propose to deal with, these mystery religions had as yet no firm hold on the indigenous people of Rome and Italy, and as they have been very elaborately treated of by competent writers of recent years, I must leave them out of these lectures. It belongs rather to the student of the first century of the Empire to try to determine the force and value of their religious or spiritual content. But I hope to prepare the way for such an enquiry by showing in my sixth lecture how the degradation of the idea of deity in the Augustan age gave these emotional cults their opportunity—the chance of winning the minds of earnest men in that age of awakening.

Let us now turn to the religion of the family, which will occupy the rest of this lecture. I expressed an opinion just now that if you had asked Cicero whether he believed in the deities of the household (*familia*) he would have answered in the affirmative. I believe, in fact, that wherever the worship of these deities survived, so far from being treated with contempt, like many of the anthropomorphised gods, they were accepted as guardian powers without questioning, in the spirit of the old Roman worship; and that the value of that spirit (which was far greater from a religious point of view than that of the State worships of the day) was thus preserved, remaining a useful asset in the religious consciousness of the people.

True, the evidence available is not of a positive character. The domestic spirits do not figure largely in the private *ex-votos* of the Corpus; even Vesta claims very few;[1] nor do they appear in the *Carmina Epigraphica*. But this simply shows that their benevolence was taken for granted without *vota*; their help was assured without negotiation: they were part of the daily life of the family, and received daily worship. That they continued to be worshipped for centuries is an ascertained fact; when the private rooms of the Roman house retreated from the front, the hearth and the domestic deities went with them, and there remained until it was thought necessary in the interest of Christianity to forbid their worship in the fourth century.[2]

I do not need here to explain the character of Vesta and the Di Penates, and their close connexion. We may say that they were originally simply the fire and the stores, conceived as having life and power, but not as spirits; but later they were thought of more animistically, *i.e.* as spirits resident in the hearth-fire and the stores. The origin of such animistic ideas still remains matter of doubt; but what is of importance for us is that this residence in the house, like that of the *numina* later on in the State, implied a friendly and benevolent character, in contrast to the very doubtful attitude of the wilder

---

[1] See De Marchi, *La Religione nella vita privata*, i. 267. The index to Buecheler's *Carmina Epigraphica* (Vesta, Genius, Penates) has nothing to help us.

[2] *The Religious Experience of the Roman People*, p. 430.

spirits beyond the house and its land. This character, reaching on into the latest Roman times, gradually, we may suppose, invested them also with the character of deities.

The word used by the Latins for this animistic conception was *deus*, which in this singular number is more familiar to us as meaning an individualised deity or *numen* of historical times. But as an anthropologist might expect, it is in the plural when we first meet with it. The spirits of the house were from the first known as *di penates*, including Vesta; so too, as we shall see directly, the spirits of the dead of the family were known as *di parentum*, later as *di Manes*. It is plain that the Latins liked to group their spirits in this way, "unter einem bestimmten Gesichtspunkte," as Wissowa puts it,[1] under a definite principle or point of view: in historical times we find this principle extended in many ways, e.g. *di coniugales, di inferi, di aquatiles*, and so on.[2] This means simply that the feeling of animism survived the individualisation of the *deus*; even in the inscriptions of the Empire we find the same tendency to pluralise the supernatural, for the Roman soldier, when he found himself in a strange and distant land, was often beset by the same doubt as to number, sex, and wishes of the spirit-world around him which had beset the early Roman agriculturist.[3] Thus the plural *di* seems of the very

[1] *Religion und Kultus der Römer*, ed. 2, p. 162.
[2] For *di conservatores*, Toutain, *Les Cultes païens dans l'Empire romain*, p. 441. For *di aquatiles* see Wissowa, *R.K.* p. 228, note 6.
[3] See an interesting passage in Toutain, i. 458. Commenting on this

DOMESTIC DEITIES

essence of animism, while the adjective added to it helps to classify the animistic conceptions, to give them that order combined with significance, which the organised Roman worship demanded.

There was, however, one spirit of the household which does not seem to have been reckoned among the Di Penates: I mean the Genius of the paterfamilias. This Genius, which calls for careful consideration because it survived and expanded in meaning all through the life of the Roman people, seems to have expressed originally (as I believe) the special idea of the mysterious power of the paterfamilias to continue the family and keep up its connexion with the *gens*.[1] The question for us is, Was it in that capacity reckoned as a *deus*? A hard question to answer, seeing that we do not know accurately the historical development of that word. But we may at any rate agree that the Genius was on the border of *deus*-land in the period we are dealing with. In Tibullus iv. 5. 9–10 a girl thus addresses the Genius of her lover on his birthday:

> Magne Geni, cape tura libens votisque faveto,
> Si modo, cum de me cogitat, ille calet;

---

habit of grouping, he says: "Essayons donc de nous représenter ce qui passait dans l'esprit et dans le cœur d'un de ses officiers, envoyés en garnison au nord de la Bretagne, le long du Rhin, ou du moyen Danube. Évidemment il se croyait relégué au bout du monde." Therefore he commends himself to the *Genius loci*, as well as to *Fortuna redux*, *Roma aeterna*, and *Fatum bonum* (*C.I.L.* vii. 370). This entirely bears out my remarks in *Religious Experience, etc.* p. 287. *Religio* arises afresh when a Roman finds himself in a region of unknown supernatural forces. If we could only also know what idea he had in his head of these deities!

[1] *Religious Experience, etc.*, p. 74 foll.

and again, line 20 :

> At tu, Natalis [*i.e.* Genius], *quoniam deus omnia sentis,*
> Adnue : quid refert, clamne palamne roget ?

Wine, life-giving and strengthening, is the regular libation to Genius ;[1] this always seems to indicate a desire to increase the vitality of the spirit thus propitiated, to make a *deus* of it, for wine, we must remember, had a mystic connexion with blood.[2] Significant, too, is the fact that the members of the household used to swear by the Genius of the head of the house ; and here the suggestion seems obvious that the appeal of this oath is to a higher or more godlike element in the paterfamilias—his soul, if we like so to call it.

Was this an immortal element, or rather, was it so thought of in this age ? This is an important question for us ; but the evidence, though interesting, is not decisive. In a well-known but difficult passage of Horace[3] Genius is described as—

> natale comes qui temperat astrum,
> Naturae deus humanae, mortalis in unum
> Quodque caput, . . .

The poet is asking what makes the difference between brothers, and answers the question by saying that only Genius knows, who controls as a companion the star of our birth, a human deity, mortal as regards the individual. He does not seem to have thought

[1] Tibull. ii. 2. 5 foll. W. Schmidt, *Geburtstag im Altertum,* p. 26.
[2] *Die sakrale Bedeutung des Weines im Altertum,* by Karl Kircher, p. 74 foll. (Giessen, 1910).
[3] *Epist.* ii. 2. 183 foll. Did Horace know the Posidonian use of δαίμων ? See below, p. 20, note 2.

of Genius as a part of the World-soul in the Stoic sense, and therefore in essence immortal; but that was an easy step onwards for Romans meditating about this mysterious spirit and becoming infected by the philosophy of the δαίμων. For Apuleius the Genius is both *deus* and *immortalis*: "is deus qui est animus suus cuique, quanquam sit immortalis, tamen quodammodo cum homine gignitur" (*de deo Socr.* 15). But in the early Empire men seem to have reckoned the Genius with the *di Manes*, as sepulchral inscriptions prove,[1] and thus must have thought of it in some sense as a soul surviving the death of the body. We may recall the fact that Cicero in the *de Finibus* (ii. 40) describes Man as " deus mortalis "; and we may perhaps conclude that the thinking Romans of his age, though they may have differed as to his immortality, thought that there was a godlike element in mortal man, for which Genius was at once a convenient word and a sufficient testimony.

But there was another sense, if I am not mistaken, in which Genius might mark continuity, if not exactly immortality, in human life and institutions. The living productive force of the paterfamilias might well be thought of as his permanent companion and protector throughout life, even before any knowledge of the Greek δαίμων had reached Rome; and in this sense of a permanent protecting power the word Genius might be extended not only to places,

[1] See a collection of these in Otto's article "Genius" in Pauly-Wissowa p. 1163.

the sense in which it is familiar to us all, but to groups of individuals, such as legions, schools, colonies, and so on. In this form it spread all over the Empire, even to remote Britain, as Dessau's selection of *tituli* relating to Genius will show at a glance.[1]

If we ask what was the idea of Genius in all these later developments, and whether it contained a notion of divinity, we may perhaps distinguish two periods. First, in the last two centuries B.C., as transferred from man to places, or to an abstraction like the *populus Romanus*, it may be taken as indicating the divine force of life and action permeating the natural world, as well as human life individual or collective. It is interesting to note that it here approaches the idea of the world-soul, as Varro seems to have seen: for St. Augustine quoting him says, " Genium dicit esse uniuscuiusque animum rationalem et ideo esse singulos singulorum, talem autem mundi animum deum esse: ad hoc idem utique revocat, *ut tanquam universalis genius ipse mundi animus esse credatur.*" [2] The words that follow also help us to understand how Genius came to be applied to the old gods, *e.g.* Genius Iovis. " Hic est igitur quem appellant Iovem. Nam si omnis genius deus, et omnis viri animus genius, *sequitur ut sit omnis viri animus deus*: quod si et ipsos abhorrere absurditas

---

[1] *C.I.L.* vii. 370: Dessau II. i. p. 85. See also the exhaustive account of Genius in the Latin provinces, in Toutain's *Cultes paiens*, ii. 439 foll.

[2] *Civ. Dei*, vii. 13. What Varro called *Genius* Posidonius called δαίμων: see the fragment from Galen quoted by Mr. Bevan, *Stoics and Sceptics*, p. 103. Presumably the idea was due to Posidonius and adapted by Varro to Roman terminology.

ipsa compellit, restat ut eum singulariter et excellenter dicant deum genium, quem dicunt mundi animum ac per hoc Iovem." Varro in this kind of syncretism had got beyond Cicero, who in his religious speculations does not trouble himself at all about Genius, forgetting his Italian treasures while pursuing foreign philosophy. He did not live to see the reversion to the Genius of an individual, as a representative of the State, to which I must return in another lecture.

Secondly, under the Empire Genius came to be ascribed to institutions in a curious way that may throw back some light upon the whole strange history of the idea. It is used not only of the senate, the plebs, and of houses and places, but of granaries and storehouses, of *macella*, of treasuries, and, lastly, even of a particular tax. *Genius venalicius* is in more than one Roman *ex-voto* the protecting or maintaining power of the tax on the sale of slaves;[1] and the devotees were probably persons engaged in the business or in collecting the tax, and whose living depended on its maintenance. How far is there in this last strange example, or in the others, still an idea of divine force at work for the good of man ? I dare not answer the question definitely : but I am tempted to think that Genius here represents that conviction of the living force (*Lebensgeist*) of the imperial government with which eventually barbarians as well as Romans became infected ; for the idea never seems to be applied to things of transient

[1] *C.I.L.* vi. 396 : Dessau 3671.

existence, *e.g.* a cohort,[1] always to permanent and highly organised institutions, like a legion or a tax or a province. Looking back from this point on the earlier history of the same idea I am inclined to see a confirmation of my conjecture that Genius in the earliest times stood for the permanent principle in social life, the continued existence of the family and the *gens* : for to permanence add the kindred idea of benevolent protection, arising when the mysterious power becomes realised as more personal, and you have almost the whole range of the concept sufficiently explained. And it will now be easy to see that in Genius, as it spread out into these many varied forms, we may well have a substantial contribution to later ideas of deity. Permanence, benevolence, and personality are all elements to be found in Genius, and I do not wonder that Varro brought him into touch with the greatest of all gods.

Lastly, we must reckon within the worship of the family the cult of the dead. Did this cult influence Roman ideas of deity in the last century B.C. ? Were the dead of the family thought of as deities in any sense ? In almost the earliest Roman document known to us they are called *di,—di parentum*, which

[1] See von Domaszewski, *Religion des römischen Heeres*, p. 103. The word Genius is not applied even to permanent cohorts, *e.g.* the praetorian, until the third century, never to the cohorts of a legion which, like maniples, had only a temporary organisation and existence. The Genius of a *centuria* was possible because the century had a permanent organisation of its own : the altars to the Genius were erected by the *signifer, optio*, and *tesserarius* of the *centuria*. See Mommsen in index to *C.I.L.* iii. p. 1161 (quoted by von Dom.). I shall return to this subject when treating of the *Genius Imperatoris*. See below, p. 132.

shows plainly that they were spirits of some sort, like the *di penates*. This document is a so-called *lex regia* attributed to Servius Tullius (Festus, 230), where it is laid down that the son who strikes his parent must be made *sacer* to the *di parentum*, *i.e.* cursed and consecrated to them;[1] thus these *di* are conceived as protecting spirits of the family, concerned equally with it in punishing the sin committed against both. But they were thought of collectively, not individually, and it may be doubted whether the offerings at the grave of an individual were really anything more than the yearly renewal of the rites of burial, which secured the dead man's peace and prevented his wandering back to the house. These are survivals from a very primitive stage of thought, and must not be taken as proving that the dead were *dei* as well as *di*, worshipped as individual deities as well as in the spirit-group. The *di parentes* are the group of the dead of the family, and the whole community of the dead, as they rested in their necropolis without the city, were *di Manes*; and in neither group was there any distinct individualisation, and therefore, so far as I can see, no progress towards a clearer idea of their divinity, for many centuries. Dr. Charles has lately shown us in his Drew Lecture (1912) that so far from theology being affected by eschatology, the reverse is really the case; and that ideas of a future life drag slowly behind the development of theological science.

[1] See *Journal of Roman Studies*, vol. i. p. 57 foll.

True, from gross and grotesque notions of ghosthood this people was saved, partly by the practice of burning the dead, to which, as archaeologists seem to agree, they were always addicted, putting no material objects in the grave for the use of the dead man:[1] partly also by the institution of the *Parentalia*, which suggests an entirely friendly feeling between the dead and their surviving kin. But if they thought of the departed as spirits (*di*), as passed from a material existence to a spiritual one, I doubt if they ever addressed them as they addressed their *numina*, seeking to make their peace with them through sacrifice and prayer,—the invariable processes of true worship. I can find no trace of sacrifice or prayer to the dead, apart from the usual offerings at the grave, which were not true sacrifices, earlier than the fifth *Aeneid*, where we find Anchises worshipped on the anniversary of his burial with altar ritual and even with prayer, *i.e.* for favourable winds.[2] But we must remember that Anchises was more than an ordinary human being,[3] and it must remain doubtful whether we can accept Virgil's picture as representing

[1] It was the same with the people of the *terremare*, probably the ancestors of the Latins; Peet, *Stone and Bronze Ages in Italy*, p. 370. Modestow, *Introduction à l'histoire romaine*, p. 195. Von Duhn, *Rückblick auf die Gräberforschung* (Heidelberg, 1911), p. 18.

[2] *Aen.* v. 45-103. There was a clear distinction in Greek religion between offerings at the grave and real sacrifices, *i.e.* between θυσίαι and ἐναγίσματα. See some interesting remarks of Mr. Lawson in his *Modern Greek Folklore and Ancient Greek Religion*, p. 530. The funeral passages in the *Aeneid* would probably repay a special investigation.

[3] Servius seems to have recognised this: in commenting on lines 47 foll. he makes it plain that the burial rites of Anchises constituted an apotheosis.

a general usage, even among the richer classes, in the last century B.C.

With the gradual individualisation of the dead, a process proved by innumerable inscriptions of the Empire, the question may arise whether there is not here an advance in what we may call the religious consciousness of the Roman, preparing him for more elevated ideas of divinity than he could draw from the degraded polytheism of his time. When the religious consciousness of the Jew deepened, after the period of the Captivity, the individual came more and more to count himself the object of God's care, to believe that he will share in the Messianic kingdom, rising from the grave as an individual being. Thus the growth of the belief in an individual existence after death seems to follow on a clearer conception of the Deity, and a closer relation to Him among the Jewish people.[1]

Can we talk of such a growth of religious consciousness in the Italy of this period? I have elsewhere endeavoured to trace it in the mind of Cicero,[2] but at the best the phrase could be applicable only to a few minds. For those few it may have affected their

---

[1] Schürer, *History of Jews in the Time of Christ*, E.T. II. ii. p. 130. A more exact account of this development is now to be found in Dr. Charles's *Drew Lecture on Immortality* (Oxford, 1912), where the limitations of individualism in the later Jewish doctrine are pointed out. The early Stoics allowed that a good man's soul might survive individually till reabsorbed into the primal fire. The later adapters of Stoicism (*e.g.* Posidonius as seen in Cic. *Tusc.* i. 40 foll., and Sext. Empir. ix. 41) put forward more definite cosmical or astronomical ideas of the experience of the *daimon* after death. See Bevan, *Stoics and Sceptics*, 108 foll.

[2] *Religious Experience, etc.*, p. 384 foll.

conception of the divine : it is, for example, closely connected with apotheosis, to which we are coming later on. But on the whole, though the question is a very difficult one, the Italian ideas about the dead in this age seem to me too indistinct to have been of any real theological value.[1] And we must not forget that at this same time the belief in immortality was by no means strong among the better educated classes. The general tendencies of the age discouraged it; Lucretius and the Epicureans ardently denied it; and the doubt which recurs again and again in the sepulchral inscriptions of the Empire probably existed unexpressed in the minds of the men of an older generation.[2]

In trying to sum up the religious value of these domestic worships we must keep in mind the fact, about which I have more to say later on, that in that

[1] They are none too distinct in the period that followed. In the *Carmina Epigraphica* we have all the more elaborate sepulchral inscriptions to be found in the *Corpus*; and the following epitaphs are selected from Buecheler's collection, as showing various aspects of the word " Manes " : 197, 215, 366, 395 (York), 428, 1029, 1117, 1155, and 1164. To these I may add the last words of the " Laudatio Turiae," *C.I.L.* vi. 1527 : " Te Di Manes tui ut quietam patiantur atque ita tueantur opto."

[2] The following expressions of doubt are culled from the *Carm. Epigr.* :—
Carm. 428, last lines (age of Hadrian) :
    Nunc tibi ne graue sit, felix quicunque uiator
    Dicere : si sapiunt aliquid post funera Manes,
    Antoni et Proculi molliter ossa cubent.
214 (Aquileia) :
    Nil mali est ubi nil est,
    Labori]s est, ut occubas, t[ibi finis.
191 (Mutina) :
    Sumus mortales, immortales non sumus.
Cp. 484, 525, 588 (these last two recalling the old myths of Hades), 1251, 1582, 1551 line 14.

age the real enemy to all inspiring ideas of the divine nature, and therefore the real enemy of religion in any true sense of the word, was the effete polytheism of the Graeco-Roman world. So too in our own day one of the first conditions of revivified Christianity must be the disappearance of that effete polytheism, the worship of local saints and local forms of the Virgin Mary, among the ignorant classes of certain parts of Europe. I think, on the whole, that the Romans had an antidote of some value against a degraded polytheism, in the domestic cults of Vesta, the Penates, Genius, and, perhaps, the dead of the family. Their worship in most households, we may believe, was not a sham, even in the last century B.C. It was regular in respect of time, and simple in its ritual. It indicated a reliance of the family, for its support and continuance, on certain manifestations of a Power beyond human control, approachable by all members of the household, and without a priestly medium to petrify it, as the Graeco-Roman gods had been petrified.

One more word before I leave the worship of the household. All these deities (if we may so call them) seem to express, however imperfectly, that idea of the continuity of Life which lies so near to that of Deity in a nobler sense; and this is possibly the reason why their vitality was so persistent. Vesta symbolised the continuity of the family life: her hearth-fire, like that of the State in historical times, had originally been kept ever burning with religious care. The Penates expressed the continuity of the household's means of subsistence; for as we are now beginning to realise, the grain, and especially the seed-corn, was in early times the object of the greatest religious anxiety, of which the memory still survives in innumerable customs of which the original purpose has long vanished.[1] The Genius expressed another side of the same idea of continuity, in the power of the head of the family to carry on its life within the *gens*. And the cult or care of the dead reflected in yet another way the feeling, strong even among primitive peoples, that death is not the extinction of life; for a belief in the continuance of life seems inherent in human nature, and as one gifted anthropologist puts it, " springs itself from the consciousness of life."[2]

[1] See Miss Harrison's *Themis*, ch. ix.; the author's article, " Mundus patet," in *Journal of Roman Studies*, vol. ii. pt. i. (1912); and Dr. Cornford's paper, "'Απαρχαί and the Eleusinian Mysteries," p. 153 of *Essays and Studies*, presented to William Ridgeway, Cambridge, 1913.

[2] Crawley, *Tree of Life*, p. 224. Cp. Frazer, *The Belief in Immortality*, i. p. 467 foll.

LECTURE II

JUPITER AND THE TENDENCY TO MONOTHEISM

THOUGH the family worship was in Cicero's day neither extinct nor meaningless, the same cannot be said with confidence of the worship of the gods of the State. Many of these gods were quite dead, and nothing shows this better than the attempts of Cicero and Varro to treat them as if they were still alive.[1] They had once been functional powers acting within a definite sphere, mainly in agricultural life and experience; and as such life and experience gradually ceased to be those of the ordinary Roman, they fell into oblivion, or survived only as the obscure objects of some still obscurer form of cult, or were absorbed by Greek anthropomorphic gods, as the host will often be absorbed by the parasite, though retaining for the most part its outward appearance. I need not here go over the list of them, or point out what changes they have suffered. Janus, Juno, Mars,

[1] Cp. Wilamowitz-Möllendorf, *Lecture on Apollo* (Oxford, 1908), p. 44: "Nothing shows more clearly how dead the gods really were, than the writers who are trying earnestly to believe in them." He is writing of the Greek gods in the time of Plutarch.

Quirinus, Neptunus and the rest,—who that knows the history and literature of the age of Cicero will maintain that under these names there was then any religious vitality remaining? Even Mars, the most characteristic and interesting *numen* of the early Roman State, has, under the disintegrating acids of Greek mythology and literature, become little more than a synonym for war: good material for rhetoric and poetry, without any power of appeal to the conscience of the community, as I will show more fully in a later lecture.[1] They have all become the objects of the scorn of Lucretius, and they are destined to be the sport of Propertius and Ovid.

One of them, however, seems to stand high above all the rest, and survives as apparently in some degree a real religious force. I wish now to ask your attention to the question whether we can see any trace of the monotheistic principle in this great deity, which might contribute in some slight degree to the pantheistic or monotheistic tendency beginning now to assert itself in the Empire generally through the writings of philosophers and mystics.

But before I speak of Jupiter himself, I wish to dwell for a moment on the evidence for the idea of one great deity surviving among uncultured or half-cultured peoples. It is all the more desirable to make this short digression here, because the idea in question is more obvious and of more importance among races that have not fully developed polytheism,

[1] See below, p. 143.

TENDENCY TO MONOTHEISM

but are, or were, rather in the stage of animism or polydaemonism, like the early Italians. For example, long ago, when reading Chantepie de la Saussaye's work on the history of religions, I was at once struck by the resemblance in many details between the religious ideas and practices of the old Romans and the Chinese.[1] I mean, of course, the old religion of China, in which there were no temples or images, few names of deities, and in which divination played an important part. Had the old Chinese any sense of a single great Power, in spite of their polydaemonism?

The Scottish missionary Ross, who has paid special attention to the old Chinese religious ideas, and has recently written a book about them, seems convinced that we must include among them some conception of a supreme divine Power. He is also convinced that it preceded the popular animism, surviving unmistakably amid the chaos of systems of belief. "The oldest forms of religion in China militate against the popular assumption that first animism and then images preceded the more spiritual monotheism of what is believed to be the most recent form assumed by religion." Documentary evidence proves that four thousand years ago there was no trace of religion of a degraded form, and that there was a distinct conception of a supreme deity, who was worshipped without temple or idol, in the open air. "Down to the present day," he tells us (writing in 1909), "the sacrificial bull is burned, and the services and devo-

[1] Vol. i. p. 240 foll.

tions of the Sovereign are paid to the Supreme in the open air. . . . As then, so now, this open-air worship is silent testimony to the belief of the Chinese that God is everywhere present, invisible and all-seeing, dwelling not in a house made with hands." [1]

Not far away from China, in the north of Borneo, we have confirmatory evidence of the survival of the monotheistic idea in an animistic people, emphasised by scientific investigators of the present day; and it is to be noticed that the people in question are probably in part of Mongolian blood, and descended from a race inhabiting southern China. Drs. Hose and McDougall, in their most valuable account of the Pagan tribes of Borneo, speak of a god more powerful than all the rest, " to whom are assigned no special or departmental functions. He seems to preside or rule over the company of lesser gods, much as Zeus and Jupiter ruled over the lesser gods of the ancient Greeks and Romans." [2] " Laki Tenangan," they add, " seems to be the supreme being of the Kayan universe. He is conceived as beneficent, and, as his title Laki implies, as a fatherly god who protects mankind. . . . He is not a tribal god . . . and in this the Kayan religion shows a catholicity which gives it a claim to very high rank among all religious systems." This means, I take it, that the idea of

[1] Ross, *The Original Religion of China*, p. 159 foll. For Japan, see the article "God" in Hastings's *Dict. of Religion and Ethics*, v. 395, by Mr. Tasaku Harada, who sees a unitary force behind the manifold exhibition are called "kaini."

[2] *The Pagan Tribes of Borneo*, vol. ii. p. 5 foll.

this god is a survival of a time when, as in China, monotheism was the belief of the people. With the advance of civilisation it would seem that monotheism has a tendency to be killed by animism, which in a settled agricultural life throws up endless shoots, becoming at last a vegetation which hides almost completely the nobler tree. It is not my business here to explain this; but I can see well enough that the more the occupations of mankind in the house and the town and on the land increase in diversity and complexity, the more likelihood there will be that a people of an originally simple monotheistic belief will spread the idea of divinity over the experience of their daily life. This spreading, we know, is exactly what happened at Rome, and apparently among other races who are at the same time agricultural and animistic.

At the Congress of the history of religions in 1908 it was maintained that even in India, where the choking growth is of polytheism and fetishism, the original worship was monotheistic; but the writer of the paper, Dr. Grierson, thinks that it was connected with the Indo-Iranian sun-worship, and survives in the cult of Vishnu, originally a form of sun-worship. It survives, also, if I understand him rightly, at the back of the mind of the religious Hindu,[1] for whom polytheism and fetishism only serve for the daily needs of the material world,[2]

---
[1] See also Hastings's *Dict.* vol. v. p. 289.
[2] *Transactions of the Congress*, vol. ii. p. 44.

and cannot give that "release" which their follower craves. That release is given through communion with a personal god, by devotional faith in the Adorable alone. "This even the poorest feels in some degree, however he may be overridden by polytheism."[1] This belief was attacked by atheistical Buddhism, and allied itself with Brahminism in self-defence. The result seems to have been that though Buddhism had to go altogether, polytheistic Brahminism got the better of the belief in the one Adorable (Bhagavat)—the infinite, eternal, full of grace—which is now almost hidden away beneath it.[2]

I will only pursue this subject a little further before I return to Jupiter and Italy. It was the profound conviction of Andrew Lang that traces of a supreme deity are to be found even among the most primitive peoples: he devoted a great part of his Gifford Lectures to this subject, and brought a great deal of evidence to bear on the point. Certainly his eye for the ideas of primitive man was always wonderfully penetrating—more so perhaps than that of any of the early anthropologists. His great point, which is of interest for us here, was that the supreme gods said to be found in Australia were not developed

[1] *Transactions of the Congress of 1908*, vol. ii. p. 44 foll.

[2] Even in the religion of the Jews the same struggle with polytheism is found; and as Jahveh became more strictly the only God in post-exilic times, the old animism cropped up again in the form of intermediate beings between God and man. (Dr. Inge in *Quarterly Review*, 1914, p. 54.)

A monotheistic idea seems to lie at the back of Mithraism, as we might expect. Mithra in the *Avesta* was the spirit of light; and thus, like Zeus and Jupiter, he was a moral power. Cumont, *Monuments*, Introduction, p. 336. Note especially that he was the deity of the oath.

out of animism, and that there the ghost-worship or the cult of ancestors invaded the possibly older religion of the supreme Father.[1] That may or may not be true, but, recently, Dr. Jevons has expressed much the same opinion. I gather from his valuable little book on the *Idea of God in Early Religions*, that he feels sure that some idea of a personality greater than human may be taken to lie at the back of both polydaemonism and fetishism (p. 30). That is, if I understand him rightly, all these later systems, which I have called the growth that chokes the idea of the Supreme, imply a belief in some divine personality. Flinders Petrie again, fresh from the enormous polytheism of ancient Egypt, insists that monotheism is the first stage traceable in theology, and uses almost the same language as Lang about it. So, too, Count Goblet d' Alviella, whose knowledge of religions is vast, seems in his Hibbert Lectures disposed to trace the Indian and Greek religious philosophy which developed the later ideas of monotheism, back to an age before the full development of polytheism.[2]

While I was preparing these lectures, I learnt from an article in the *Archiv für Religionswissenschaft* that an Italian scholar, Dr. Pettazzoni, claims to have discovered a supreme deity in the island of Sardinia.

[1] *The Making of Religion*, p. 206. The evidence, however, as to the real notions of these Australian tribes is still uncertain; my friend Dr. Baldwin Spencer assures me that Lang was mistaken.

[2] Jevons, *The Idea of God in Early Religions* (Cambridge, 1911), p. 30; Petrie, *Religion of Egypt* (Constable), chap. i.; Goblet d' Alviella, *Hibbert Lectures*, p. 218 foll.

His facts and the argument he bases on them are fully set forth in a book published in 1912, *La Religione primitiva in Sardegna*. The evidence is both literary and archaeological, and the author is well acquainted with the best anthropological works of the day. I am not so sure, however, that he has really found in Sardus Pater a deity who was "the centre and sum of all religious belief and practice" (p. xvii), or who can fitly be compared to Jahveh of the Israelites. But it may be true that this mysterious deity was really the ideal of the proto-Sardian race, who survived all invasions and conquests as the father, leader, and hero of the Sardinian people (pp. 91, 194). I gladly draw attention to this work of Dr. Pettazzoni, though I cannot feel sure that his evidence, taken by itself, would have inevitably suggested the far-reaching conclusion he bases on it. For him, however, Sardus Pater "is the centre and fulcrum of all the indigenous beliefs of the island"; and "when his figure rises above the religious horizon, all the pre-existing phantoms seem to vanish, or rather to melt, in his light."[1]

But apart from this possibility of a supreme god so near as Sardinia, the reports and theories I have been alluding to suggest that in ancient Italy, where, when we first know anything about it, polydaemonism best describes the prevalent religious belief, we may quite reasonably look for some trace of a supreme deity in the background of Italian thought. And I need not say that if this is to be found anywhere, it

[1] *Archiv für Religionswissenschaft*, 1913, p. 329.

will be found in Jupiter, the Father of Heaven, and giver of all heavenly light.

We know that the Latin Jupiter was the deity of, or consisting in, the light and the heaven, and we know that he represents the same form of religious conception that is found, as the god of sky and thunder, among all Aryan peoples. As a conception of the Latin race we cannot indeed trace him to an earlier point than the settlement of the Latins in Latium, for their ancestors of the pile-dwellings and the terremare farther north in Italy have left us no certain trace of their religion. But the fact that he is found in many parts of Italy besides Latium makes it almost certain that they had him with them from the beginning, and settled him, when they settled down themselves, on some lofty hill open to the sky, with his favourite groves of oak trees clothing the slopes below him. In Latium his chief home was of course the Alban Mount, where he must have long reigned over the Latin tribes in a temple not made with hands, before the Etruscans came and built him a temple of stone. He was their supreme god, a Power, if not actually a Person, who presided over the league of Latin cities, and held them together by the strong moral bond of good faith, and the religious bond of a sacramental meal. Both these bonds are most important as showing that this great Father of the Latin stock was a far greater force with his people than the many functional *numina* whom they may have already begun to worship in their particular cities. Let us take first the sacramental meal.

I wrote in my *Roman Festivals* (p. 96) that the features of this festival, the *feriae Latinae*, betray its origin in the pastoral age. " The offerings are characteristic rather of a pastoral than an agricultural age, and suggest an antiquity that is fully borne out by the ancient utensils dug up on the Alban Mount." [1] We hear of milk offerings, but there is no mention of wine. The victim was a white heifer that had never felt the yoke, and if we accept a suggestion of Robertson Smith's, this white victim may be a reminiscence of some primitive breed of sacred white cattle. This was the chief offering, and in historical times the sacrificer was the Roman consul, a fact which proves that the head of the State, whoever he was, must have taken the same part in the earlier dim history of the Latins. The flesh was divided among the deputies of all the Latin cities, who thus placed themselves in some mystic relation with their great divinity, at the same time renewing the solemn covenant of alliance with each other. " We are here in the presence of the oldest and finest religious conception of the Latin race, which yearly acknowledges its common kinship of blood, and seals it by partaking in the common meal of a sacred victim, thus entering into communion with the god, the victim, and each other."

I said that the head of the State, whoever he was, offered the sacrifice in early times. Was not

---

[1] See Modestow, *Introduction à l'histoire romaine*, p. 253.

TENDENCY TO MONOTHEISM

this really the priest of Jupiter, the Flamen Dialis of Roman history, whose extraordinary series of disabling taboos shows that he must have been too precious to have been other than that head? I mention him here because nothing can better show the supremacy of the god than this marvellous value attributed to his priest.[1] If the priest whose duty it was to sacrifice to this great god of the race was hedged in by these innumerable taboos, then the deity to whom he sacrificed, with whom he communicated through sacrifice on behalf of the race, must have been one by the side of whom the ordinary *numen* sank into comparative insignificance. Here let me remind you that one of these taboos forbade the Flamen to take an oath. What oath was he likely to take but one by his own deity? Yet, as he was the representative of that deity among his people, or possibly in some sense personated him, he could no more take such an oath than the god could swear by himself. But let me turn for a moment to this matter of the Jupiter oath, which is also of importance as showing the supreme character of the deity.

The connexion of Jupiter with the oath is one of the earliest facts in Latin civilisation; the oath of the Fetials, *per Iovem lapidem*, is the oldest example known to us in Italy of this religious rite. I need

[1] For the view that the origin of Deity may be found in "medicine-men" of the type of this Flamen (a view for which I can find no substantial evidence), see, *e.g.*, Professor Gilbert Murray, in *Anthropology and the Classics*, p. 76. He seems to be basing his belief on Mr. Hartland's remarks in *Transactions of the Congress of Religions for 1908*, vol. i. p. 25; but Mr. Hartland refers, not to an actual, but an ideal or mythical medicine-man.

not dwell here on the peculiar ritual of this oath; I wish rather to point out the real ethical importance of it, and the proof which it contributes to our idea of the power for good of the supreme god of the sky— a power which seems to be latent in him wherever he is found, even if it be not visible at a glance. Professor Tenney Frank has lately insisted [1] that the oath, as first described by Livy (i. 32), in which the Fetials declare that the offending nation is unjust—"illum iniustum esse neque ius persolvere"—is not, as some have imagined, a mere legal formula in which *iustum* has a merely technical meaning, but has a true ethical content; and I think he is right. When private war gives place to State influence, and the normal condition of things is no longer war but peace (*hostis* losing its primitive sense of stranger), it is to the Heaven-god that the Romans appeal to sanction good faith and to punish wrong. So, too, with the other Fetial oath with the *silex*: "If the Roman people break this treaty, then do thou Jupiter so strike down the Roman people as I now strike this offering, and so much harder as thou art stronger." Long after these old practices had fallen out of use, the oath by the Heaven-god remained as the most important oath known to the State, that of the magistrate on entering office; in which with Jupiter were united the public Penates representing human life in the city. If private individuals could not usually swear by so formidable a deity, they could at least do so by that

[1] *Classical Philology*, vol. vii. No. 3.

Dius Fidius who seems beyond doubt to be another form or offshoot of the same god; and *mediusfidius* became a familiar phrase of common speech. What is really the connexion of the Sky-god with oaths? Is it not that, as Dr. Westermarck suggests,[1] he is thought of as all-seeing, one from whom no secrets can be hid; in fact a supreme god, descended perhaps from a monotheistic god? He is a witness to the taking of the oath, for he cannot be looking the other way at the time: as Cicero puts it in the *de Officiis*[2] (iii. 44), "Cum iurato sententia dicenda sit, meminerit deum se habere testem": only that in the spirit of his own age Cicero explains the god here as the swearer's own mind or conscience ("qua nihil homini dedit deus divinius"), a passage which I may refer to again in another context. This is, I imagine, why these solemn oaths were taken out in the open, so as not to hide away from the All-seeing. When you swore by Dius Fidius in ordinary life, it was proper for you to go out of the house; and Plutarch has preserved for us the custom of making boys go outside even when they wanted to say *mehercule*—which is, I think, only a later application of the old principle to a new deity.[3] It shows the conservatism of the Roman household in matters apparently small but in reality of deep significance, and helps to explain the remarkable feeling for good faith among the Romans, which made them elevate Fides, after their

[1] *Origin and Development of Moral Ideas*, vol. ii. p. 122.
[2] Bk. iii. 44.
[3] *Quaest. Rom.* 28. See *Roman Festivals*, p. 138.

manner with such abstractions, into a deity in close touch with Jupiter, if not an emanation from his being.[1]

The practical result for the Roman of this idea of the Heaven-god as the Power sanctioning the oath was immense; for the whole fabric of the State and its government, as well as its international relations, were ultimately based upon it. To understand fully the weight of the magisterial oath one must have a large knowledge of Roman *Staatsrecht*, and it would take me out of my province if I were to enlarge on it now. I think it would not be difficult to show that the Romans had a more lively sense of the sanctity of the oath than is vouchsafed to most peoples; Polybius himself was of this opinion (vi. 56). The original penalty of the false swearer had been death: "periurii paena divina exitium," says Cicero,[2] "humana dedecus." I doubt whether even in the careless age of the late Republic the *religio* of the oath had been seriously weakened. The military sacramentum continued to have full force, though it had immediate reference to the general rather than to the State. This is well illustrated in the story told by Caesar (*B.C.* ii. 28 ff.) of the scruples of the soldiers serving under Curio, who had sworn obedience to their Pompeian general before they surrendered to Caesar at Corfinium, and now were easily persuaded that they ought not to be

---

[1] Wissowa, *R.K.* ed. 2, p. 133 foll. *Roman Festivals*, p. 237.
[2] *De Legibus*, ii. 22.

fighting on Caesar's side. The speech which Caesar puts into the mouth of Curio to relieve their anxiety is worth careful study in connexion with the force of the oath at this time. Livy is reflecting the ideas of his own age when he makes Scipio speak of *periurium* in the field as affecting not only the false swearer himself, but " signa militaria et aquilas, sacramentique religionem." [1] Throughout the period of the Empire the same ideas held good.

I may seem to have been wandering away from my main theme in this lecture, but I have been trying to show that the civilising power of the oath, and with it the elevation of the conception of truth and good faith, is not due to any deity but the Heaven-god as a god supreme, in whose presence you could not safely lie or forswear yourself. As Westermarck says,[2] the habit of oath-taking has in some cases made it prudential for men to speak the truth under all circumstances.

I will add one or two remarks before I leave Jupiter and return to the writers of the Ciceronian age. If we are ready to allow that this great god of the Latins had been for many ages a supreme god, under whose sanction and protection were the federation of Latin cities and then the conduct of the Roman State, we can perhaps better understand why, when the yoke of the Etruscan was cast off, the Jupiter of the Capitol became Jupiter Optimus Maximus. These cult-titles are almost inexplicable by any analogy

[1] Livy xxvi. 48. 12.   [2] *Op. cit.* ii. 123.

known to us in the Mediterranean world of that day; I have said something about them in my Gifford Lectures (p. 238). The immediate object may have been to impress on the mind of the worshipper the fact that even the Jupiter of the Alban hill was now superseded by him of the Capitol; yet my feeling is that these titles could never have been invented but for a deity who was felt to overshadow all others, the ancestral inheritance of the race as none other was, and the one on whom the State and all individuals within it depended for their very existence, moral and material.

Again, if in Jupiter is contained a reminiscence of a supreme deity of the Latin race, we can better understand why he alone, in contrast with other deities, finds a place in the calendar of every month, on the day of the full moon; the ides of all months were great festivals of this deity, festivals as important as those of any deity not so often honoured. And once more, we can now reconcile ourselves better to the view, long held by myself and now at last accepted by Wissowa in the new edition of his great work, that Jupiter stands alone, without attachment to any female deity: that the old delusion that Jupiter and Juno were husband and wife must now be definitely abandoned as non-Italian.[1] Lastly, we may remember how easily this deity provided the

---

[1] No doubt the cult of Juno on the Kalends of each month (Wissowa, *R.K.* ed. 2, p. 186 foll.) suggests a deity in some way connected with the moon and light; but I agree with Wissowa, p. 187, that this character is derived from her relation to women.

means for the transference of the cosmical gods of the East to Italy in the second and third centuries A.D. "Optimus Maximus Caelus aeternus Iuppiter," "Iuppiter Optimus Maximus summus exsuperantissimus," "Divinarum humanarumque rerum rector fatorumque arbiter,"[1] such titles as these, attached to the old name as early as the latter half of the second century, suggest a still surviving subconscious sense of the supremacy of the old Italian god.

I may be wrong, but it is my conviction that the intensely conservative Roman mind could never, even under the domination of Etruscan and Greek religious ideas, have lost the sense of a great Power in the universe, summing up as it were the varied powers of their *numina*. I think it quite possible that this sense was always in the background of the Italian mind, as was suggested to me many years ago by a comment of H. Jordan's on the strange Fortuna-Jupiter cult of Praeneste:[2] "Non desunt vestigia divinum numen Italis notum fuisse deis deabusque omnibus et hoc ipso in quo vivimus mundo antiquius." If so cautious a scholar as Jordan could go so far as this, we need not hesitate to guess that such a *divinum numen* might remain as part of the

[1] Wissowa, *R.K.* ed. 2, p. 365. Cumont in *Archiv*, 1906, p. 323 foll., especially 332 and notes.

[2] *Roman Festivals*, p. 168. This is almost exactly the language used in the second and third centuries of Jup. Exsuperantissimus: see the commentator on Apuleius quoted by Cumont, *Archiv*, 1906, p. 332. In this connexion it may be as well to note the epithet Jovius as applied in Umbria to other deities: see *Tab. Iguv.* vi., vii. As I have said in the *Companion to Latin Studies*, p. 164, the *numen* of Jupiter seems to invade or qualify that of other deities.

subconscious equipment of the Italian mind, though rarely realised. If so, it may have made the task of Italian thinkers easier in the last century before Christ, when they broke with the imported polytheism of their Greek conquerors, and began to look about for some explanation of life and the universe which should not involve them in vulgar absurdities. Such men were Lucretius, Cicero, and Varro, who all in different ways show the same tendency to abandon or explain away the popular polytheism.

In Lucretius's case this was of course far more than a tendency; it was a dogmatic conviction that man has really no use for gods at all, great or little. Even Jupiter is to be banished with the rest. Lucretius's Jupiter is indeed not so much the Roman as the Etruscan idea of the god, upon whom he pours out a scorn that reminds us of Elijah and the prophets of Baal (vi. 387 foll.):

> Denique cur nunquam caelo iacit undique puro
> Iuppiter in terras fulmen sonitusque profundit ?
> An simul ac nubes successere, ipse in eas tum
> Descendit, prope ut hinc teli determinet ictus ?

Why, that is, is he obliged to take advantage of clouds, to come near and get a better aim at us?

Why, again asks the poet, does he smite the holy temples of the gods and break in pieces their beautifully wrought images, stripping even his own of honour with his wanton wound? Yet in spite of this it is worth while to ask the question whether there is any sign even in Lucretius of the subconscious feeling of which I have been speaking.

No word of his, it is true, actually admits the existence either of a personal or impersonal omnipotent deity. *Rerum natura* absorbs all the adoration of his soul, save what he can spare for those almost divine men who have expounded it, Empedocles and Epicurus. Yet one who has studied his poem scientifically declares that it forces on him the conviction of a mighty power behind the clashing atoms, a Power working things both terrible and lovely, but caring nought indeed for man.[1] The writer of these words may be unconsciously biassed; but to me also it seems impossible that a Roman should have been able to throw off entirely the idea of a Power manifesting itself in the universe—a power, forceful, living, full of *will*[2]—and to fill its place with an entirely mechanical theory of things. The poem is full of expressions of life and force, as are also, in a quieter tone and mode of expression, the Georgics of his successor. Think of " vivida ·vis animi," or the " *avidus* complexus " of the aether (v. 470), or the life of the earth, " partibus aeriis mundi quibus insita

---

[1] Masson, *Lucretius*, vol. i. p. 153 note. When in bk. v. 1204 foll. Lucretius shows that he understands the feeling of the Deist, who looks up at the heaven, and realises the " deum immensa potestas," he shows also, almost beyond doubt, that he had had that experience himself. See Glover, *Conflict of Religions in the Roman Empire*, p. 26.

[2] In one passage at least he expresses himself like a Roman about this Power:
  " Nec divina satum genitalem numina cuiquam
   Absterrent, pater a gnatis ne dulcibus unquam
   Appelletur," etc. (iv. 1233).

vivit" (v. 537), or the stars feeding themselves (v. 523): but every reader of Lucretius will recall a hundred passages of this kind. For him, as for Virgil, animated nature was full of life and force, because that was the essential Italian view of nature, as indeed it is that of all peoples who have reached the animistic stage, and never entirely deserted it.

Of course, when Lucretius is following his teachers, he loses for the moment the inherited instinct for forceful *numina*, or a single *numen* with will, giving life: he is too busy with fitting the atomic theory into his hexameters, and with admiring its completeness. It wholly satisfies him as against the anthropomorphic gods and their foolish ways; but it is not so easy to shake off the idea of a great *Numen*—it remains in the inner chambers of the mind.

Thus it is that we find such a strange surprise at the outset of the poem as the invocation to Venus Genetrix. Lucretius betrays himself a Roman in the first two words of the poem, "Aeneidum genetrix;" but far more, I think, in the life and force pervading the passage, and in the extraordinary twenty-first line, which makes Love the sole mistress of *Rerum Natura* ("quoniam rerum naturam sola gubernas"). He seems to say: I am going in this book to deal with the essential problem of life, production and reproduction, and Venus, as the reputed ancestor of the Romans, and of Memmius, and the ruler of the principles of reproduction, will be a suitable recipient of a conventional *invocatio*. It is curious that the

TENDENCY TO MONOTHEISM

old Italian Venus is quite possibly related in some way now lost to us to the old Italian Fortuna,[1] and as we shall see in the next lecture, Fortuna in Lucretius is hardly more than another word for Natura, and must mean some great universal force which the poet will not refer to a deity because of his intense hatred of the popular idea of the divine. I cannot help thinking that this hatred moves him even more than his mechanical theory of the world and of the origin of life.[2] The poet and the philosopher seem often to be struggling for the mastery in Lucretius, and though the poet is suppressed during great parts of the work, he asserts himself surprisingly here and there, and when he does so, betrays the inherited instinct to refer the nature of things to a forceful Will, which many might call a deity (cp. v. 1204).

I pass to a very different thinker, an ordinary human being compared with Lucretius, with much of the Italian religious feeling hidden away in him, in spite of his rhetorical and philosophical training. What view did Cicero take of the old and the new theology, and their relation to each other ? He was, of course, entirely out of touch with the Epicurean ideas of deity, and greatly preferred the Stoic elastic monism, because it was capable of being adapted without violence even to the political polytheism in which Cicero had been brought up, *a fortiori* also to the more spiritual pandaemonism which still lurked

---

[1] Wissowa, ed. 2, p. 258.   [2] Cp. *e.g.* i. 930 foll., 1020 foll.

in odd corners of the Italian mind. His account of this Stoic theology is to be read by every one in the second book of his *de Natura Deorum*, which has an unusual interest for us as almost certainly reproducing the views of Posidonius,[1] who is generally believed to have greatly modified the traditional Stoic orthodoxy.

I need not here attempt to explain what that orthodoxy was; it has been recently well treated by Mr. Arnold in his *Roman Stoicism*, on the basis of the Stoic fragments so carefully collected by von Arnim, with which may be compared the 16th and 17th lectures of the late Dr. Caird's *Evolution of Theology in the Greek Philosophers*. What concerns us here is the light in which Cicero and Posidonius thought of the Stoic deity.

At the beginning of his second book Cicero describes this deity in a magnificent phrase, which seems to embody at once the best of Greek philosophy and of Roman religion: " Numen praestantissimae mentis " (the will of a supreme mind). Here he seems even to catch something of the spirit of the astral religion which Professor Cumont has lately traced back at Rome to Posidonius; for it is when we look up at the sky and contemplate the heavenly bodies that this idea of God, according to Cicero, should arise in our minds. But in the next sentence he suddenly transfers the idea to the great Roman deity, quoting his favourite line from Ennius,

[1] See last lecture, p. 2.

TENDENCY TO MONOTHEISM

"Aspice hoc sublime candens quem invocant omnes Iovem." True, this transference is as old as Stoicism itself, and in one sense far older; for the Greeks had never hesitated to compare or identify their divine product of philosophy with the supreme heaven-god of their race. But for Cicero is Jupiter here only an interpreting literary expression, or could a Roman really think of him as Panaetius or Posidonius could think of Zeus, or as long ago Cleanthes had thought of that Zeus in his famous hymn?[1]

Cicero was undoubtedly fond of using the name of Jupiter to represent the Stoic deity. Many years before the *de Natura Deorum* was written, when drawing the Roman constitution against a background of Stoic principles, he had spoken of Jupiter in Homeric phrase as king of gods and men, as ruler and father of all. And in the second book of the *Laws* he defined law as "ratio recta summi Iovis."[2] And by Jupiter he really means the Roman deity, though he may be thinking of him more or less in the character of Zeus; for when Cotta in *de Natura Deorum*, iii. sec. 11, is criticising the Stoic phrase I quoted just now ("numen praestantissimae mentis," as suggested by the open heaven), he alludes to the difficulty of connecting the deity thus splendidly char-

---

[1] The question seems to be answered in Cicero's *Somnium Scipionis*, xiii. 13. The *princeps deus*, *i.e.* Jupiter, can be thought of by a Roman as ruling over social and political life, which depends on him for its maintenance. "Nihil est enim illi principi deo qui omnem hunc mundum regit ... acceptius, quam concilia coetusque hominum iure consociati, quae civitates appellantur."

[2] *de Legibus*, ii. 10 *fin.*, *Rep.* i. 56.

acterised with the one who resides on the Capitol: "quasi verum quisquam nostrum istum potius quam Capitolinum Iovem appellet."[1] Varro, I may observe, at this same time found no difficulty in the identification.[2] St. Augustine quotes him as holding that the Romans had dedicated the Capitol to Jupiter, who by his spirit breathes life into everything in the universe. He even identifies this Jupiter with the god of the monotheistic peoples of the East, and in particular with the God of the Jews.[3]

In spite, then, of Cotta's criticism from the academic point of view—in which it must be allowed that he puts his finger on a weak point—there were two reasons why such a bold descent should be possible for a Roman from the *sublime candens* or the πνεῦμα νοερὸν καὶ πυρῶδες of the Stoics to his own little hill within the walls of Rome.

One reason lies in the Roman conception of the Jupiter of the Capitol as the builder-up of the Roman empire, that astonishing fact for which Polybius found it hard to account, and which was soon to inspire the poet of the *Aeneid*, who deliberately made this deity into a "numen praestantissimae mentis," protecting and controlling the destinies of the Roman world. In this sense he could be conceived as almost, in Stoic language, a creative intelligence, caring for

[1] Cp. Seneca, *Nat. Quaest.* ii. 45, quoted by Arnold, *Roman Stoicism*, p. 221. Mayor's *N.D.* iii. p. 68 should be consulted.

[2] See my *Social Life in Rome*, p. 337. Add Lucan ix. 578 foll.

[3] Varro, *Ant. Div.* (Agahd), pp. 149, 163 (fragm. 156-158, 204-205), 188. Note that Jupiter was not, like most polytheistic deities, emptied of his old content in the Rome of this age.

mankind. I believe that if we could get to the back of Cicero's mind, we should find him capable of being satisfied with this interpretation of the Stoic universal Reason; and I do not see that any Stoic could be hurt by it. The Jupiter of the Capitol seemed to rule over the civilised world; this is the meaning of the many imitation Capitols, if we may so call them, which are found at this time and later in many cities of the empire. I may refer you to the most recent and careful account of these in M. Toutain's work, *Les Cultes païens dans l'empire romain*, vol. iii. p. 183 foll., and to the collection he has made of the epigraphical evidence for the spread of the cult of the great *numen* over the Latin provinces of the west. This deity was not for small things and small people, but for great ones; there is a breadth and range about his action which exceeds that of any Graeco-Roman god, for he is indeed the reflection of the greatness of his people, the religious interpretation of their amazing strength.

The other reason lies in the fact that the Stoics, who thus helped to elevate the Roman's idea of his deity, were themselves constantly hovering on the verge of a divine personality. Mr. Arnold has well remarked that of the Stoic arguments for the existence of a god or gods[1] the first two and most important seem to substitute for the abstract term " providence " the more concrete and (as we should phrase it) the more personal conception of a deity. Certainly the

[1] Arnold, *op. cit.* p. 218.

later Stoics, and Posidonius in particular, were apt to slide back from the abstract Stoic unity into something of the old Platonic dualism. God, the guide and ruler of the world, is to them sometimes distinct from the world, though they always claim the right to assert that the world and all within it is divine, in virtue of the divine principle pervading it.[1]

Thus as the Roman might work up from his Jupiter of the Capitol to the lofty Stoic conception of a "numen praestantissimae mentis," so the Stoic himself would not find it inconsistent with his principles to work down from that divine Reason to a deity seated in the Roman Capitol and controlling the destinies of the world. And now we may begin to see how, through this combination of Roman imperial *numen* with Stoic universal Reason, the idea of deity in this period shows a tendency to become monotheistic.[2] I am disposed to think that this tendency was of great value in the generations to come.

[1] Varro, *Ant. Div.* p. 149 (Agahd).

[2] It may be interesting to compare this tendency with a similar one (though not by any means so in all respects) which we meet with in the syncretism of three or four centuries later. See Toutain, *op. cit.* vol. ii. p. 227, and especially the quotation from J. Réville on p. 228.

LECTURE III

COSMIC IDEAS OF DEITY

WHILE considering in the last lecture the tendency to see a monotheistic principle in the *numen* of Jupiter, and in the reception given him by Roman Stoics as the supreme god of light and heaven, you may have noticed that I said nothing of the Sun, the most obvious, useful, and important of the light-giving bodies, which three centuries later became the centre of an imperial monotheistic worship. This seems the place to say what need here be said about it.

Sun-worship, it is true, has been far less widely distributed than one would expect. For example, in the last really important book about peoples in a condition midway between savagery and civilisation, (whose religious ideas always seem to me of especial interest for classical students), the *Pagan Tribes of Borneo*, by Hose and McDougall, it is not even mentioned, though the sun plays a powerful part in the lives of the people. There seems to be no sure trace of it in the old religion of China: the monotheistic element there is not distinctly related to it. In ancient Babylonia the moon is the chief deity, and in comparing Babylon and Greece Dr. Farnell has nothing to tell us about the sun.[1] As Cumont remarks, in hot countries the sun is an enemy against whom you seek to protect yourself: the people of the burning plains of Mesopotamia preferred the soft light of the moon, which illuminated without damaging them, to the fierce star whose heat dried up the earth and wasted the human body. The moon is in fact, as he points out, a much more useful star for the human race in such climates. Sun-worship has been, he adds, the work of astronomers, and the prestige of the sun has increased with increasing knowledge of him. It is essentially " un culte savant " : it developed with the growth of science, and reached its zenith in the old world when astronomical knowledge was at its highest point. Where science did not advance, as in Egypt, in spite of some attempts to set up the sun, the moon retained her supremacy.[2]

Whether there ever was a real sun-worship in Italy, apart from that of Jupiter and the Heaven generally, has been a disputed question. Two facts are, however, quite certain : (1) That Sol is not to be found in the oldest Roman religious calendar, nor do any of the most ancient priesthoods betray a connexion with sun-worship; (2) There is no certain trace of sun-worship in Italy : the god Soranus of

---

[1] *Greece and Babylon*, by L. R. Farnell (Wilde Lectures for 1911).
[2] Cumont, *Théologie solaire*, p. 3 foll. I am not sure that M. Cumont had considered the sun-worship of Mexico and Peru. After reading Viscount Bryce's *Travels in South America*, I am led to suppose that sun-worship in Peru was due to a *want* of sunshine during a great part of the year.

Soracte, taken by Preller and Mannhardt for the Sun on the ground of an alleged etymology, is plainly only an adjectival form of a place-name.[1] Wissowa seems to have shown that neither Sun nor Moon were thought of as deities until certain Greek coin-types, with a *quadriga* and a *biga* for sun and moon respectively, came to Rome in the Second Punic War and invited imitation, producing in later times a special connection of Sol with the Circus.[2] Varro indeed asserts that these cults were of Sabine origin, and brought to Rome by the Sabine king Tatius;[3] and there really was a cult of Sol, with a *pulvinar*, on the Quirinal Hill, the traditional Sabine settlement, hard by the temple of Quirinus. But the mention of the *pulvinar* seems to prove that the cult was of Greek or Etruscan origin, and comparatively late. Again there is a Sol Indiges mentioned in three calendars, though not inscribed in the large capitals which mark the oldest calendar of all; his seat was also on the Quirinal, and the cult may be the same as that just mentioned. The cult-title Indiges is best explained as added in the Augustan age to distinguish this Sol from foreign sun-deities now beginning to find their way to Rome.[4] On the

---

[1] See, *e.g.*, Mannhardt, *Wald- und Feldkulte*, p. 330 foll.; Wissowa, *R.K.* ed. 2, p. 238. In Etruria there is no sign of an important sun-god; in the liver of Piacenza Usil is not in any of the *regiones*, nor does Martianus Capella so mention him: see Thulin, *Die Götter des Martianus Capella*, p. 18.

[2] Wissowa, *R.K.* ed. 2, p. 315; *Myth. Lex.* s.v. "Sol," p. 1138. Both sun and moon might have been included in the great Father of Heaven.

[3] Varro, *L.L.* v. 68, 74.

[4] Wissowa, *R.K.* ed. 2, p. 317.

whole it seems pretty plain that the old Roman stock had no need for a sun-cult, and we may suppose that the climate was not so hot as to suggest placation of the sun, nor so rainy and cloudy as to compel them to pray for his aid.

But in Cicero's time we can just trace a beginning of that recognition of the sun as a great god, which became more obvious under Augustus, and eventually swept the Empire. The importance of this fact in the history of Roman worship has recently been pointed out by Cumont, both in his *Théologie solaire* and in his lectures on Astrology and Religion.[1] In the opinion of this unrivalled investigator of religion in the imperial period, the recognition of the Sun at Rome was originally due to Posidonius,[2] who fascinated the Graeco-Roman world by the reach and brilliancy of his theories, widening the narrow channel of Stoic thought, and letting into it fresh currents of oriental and astrological origin. The sun had meanwhile become a great god in the Orient, and especially the god of kings—himself the king of all other stars. He ruled their courses; Varro in this very age expressed this view: "sol . . . qui stellas ipsas quibus movemur permovet."[3] The same idea, that the sun

---

[1] *Astronomy and Religion among the Greeks and Romans*, p. 133 foll.; *Théologie solaire du paganisme romain*, p. 27 foll.

[2] But Cleanthes had anticipated Posidonius: Cic. *Acad.* ii. 126, "Cleanthes, qui quasi maiorum est gentium Stoicus, Zenonis auditor, solem dominari et rerum potiri putat." Zeno and Cleanthes differed, the former maintaining that the aether was "summus deus," while Cleanthes supported the claim of the sun. See Arnold, *Roman Stoicism*, p. 184.

[3] *Ap.* Censorinum *de Die Natali*, 8.

was ruler of the heavens, crops up here and there in Cicero, *e.g.* in *de Div.* ii. 89, where it may reflect an opinion of Panaetius. Cumont lays great stress on words in the *Somnium Scipionis* (sec. 4) to the same effect: "mediam regionem sol obtinet, dux et princeps et moderator luminum reliquorum." In such passages the root idea seems to be that the sun was to the other heavenly bodies much what we understand by gravitation now. But the other idea of the sun's benevolent influence on earth is not forgotten, and is also found in Cicero, as indeed we might expect. Thus we find "sol, qui astrorum obtinet principatum"[1] in direct relation to the earth as light-giver. So for Pliny a century later the sun is "principale naturae regimen ac numen."[2] In this way the sun soon reached the position of an intelligent power (φῶς νοερόν)—*dux et princeps*, as Cicero called him, words which imply intelligence; offering himself, as it were, to the Stoics for recognition as their Reason or Soul of the world instead of Zeus or Jupiter. It was still a far cry from this to the Sol Invictus of the later empire, who is creator and saviour of man, a personal god in a sense which could hardly be admitted by the Stoics. Yet the influence of sun-worship on Stoicism is a fact, and as far as Rome is concerned, it is due to Posidonius through the writings of Cicero and Varro. But whether either

---

[1] *N.D.* ii. 49 and 102. The word "principatus" is incidentally interesting here as it was now beginning to be applied to the supremacy of a ruler at Rome, *e.g.* in Cic. *Fam.* i. 9. 21.
[2] *Hist. Nat.* ii. 12.

of these three could bring himself to think of the sun as the one supreme god, and so to displace Jupiter, may fairly be doubted. We cannot say more than that they took a step in that direction.[1]

In the Augustan age (though Cumont has not noticed this) I think we can trace a more definite tendency to think of the sun as a powerful deity. I referred just now to Sol Indiges, and to Wissowa's explanation of it, which reminds us that foreign solar worship was coming in at this time. But apart from Mithras, we have the fact [2] that Augustus brought two obelisks from Egypt and dedicated them to the sun-god: both are still standing in Rome. Again, the Apollo of Augustus is really the sun, and the *quadriga* on his temple of Apollo was recognised as belonging to the sun through the Greek coins mentioned above. I may also note that special attention had been called to the sun by the eclipse that followed Caesar's assassination, to which Virgil refers at the end of the first *Georgic*:

> Sol tibi signa dabit. Solem quis dicere falsum
> Audeat ? ille etiam caecos instare tumultus
> Saepe monet, fraudemque et operta tumescere bella.
> Ille etiam extincto miseratus Caesare Romam,
> Cum caput obscura nitidum ferrugine texit,
> Impiaque aeternam timuerunt saecula noctem.[3]

And we must not forget that in the fourth *Eclogue*

---

[1] Cumont, *Th. solaire*, p. 28 foll., explains the difficulty they would have to meet.

[2] *C.I.L.* vi. 701-2. The chariot of the sun is also on the corslet of the Prima Porta statue of Augustus.   [3] *Georg.* i. 463 foll.

the last age was to be that of Apollo, whose reign was even then beginning ("tuus iam regnat Apollo"); and Servius, commenting on this line, says that according to the Sibyl this last age was that of the sun, thus identifying by inference the sun and Apollo. But I must here leave sun-worship, which was as yet only beginning in Italy.

Before I pass in my next lecture to a different aspect of the subject I have taken in hand, I must deal with another form of belief or speculation, which at this time is beginning to be of importance. Whether it means belief in a deity, or speculation as to the existence of some mysterious cosmic force,[1] is the question which I want to discuss in the rest of this lecture. No doubt you will have noticed, in the literature of the Ciceronian and Augustan periods, the frequent allusion to Fortuna as a power in human life. It seems to me much more prominent than any use we make in these days of the influence of chance or luck. Not only individuals, but all philosophical schools and all historians, were constantly talking about Fortuna or τύχη, and the question for us is what they meant by these names.

Was this Fortuna a deity in any sense, or did she supply the place of a deity, for the Romans of the late Republic and early Empire? To answer this

[1] Dr. Bussell has some remarks in his book on Marcus Aurelius, p. 43, which are of interest here: "The course of the world might be called providential, in a vague and general sense; but the parts, the special events, were abandoned to the usurper fortune."

question I must glance at the previous history of Fortuna at Rome.

We first meet with Fortuna as a Latin, though not a Roman deity. Her name is formed adjectivally from *fors*; and *fors*, so far as we know, must have meant luck, *i.e.* the incalculable element in human life, working either for the good or harm of man. We must not suppose that this meant a capricious force, but simply the idea of luck or accident which is common to the mind and language of all peoples, whether educated to think or not. Fortuna was the *numen* presiding over this incalculable element in human life; and this connotation she never perhaps entirely lost. But she is always, until the very end of the republican period, to be distinguished from blind chance, for which the word is usually *temeritas*: thus in some famous lines of Pacuvius—

> Sunt etiam alii philosophi qui contra *Fortunam* negant
> ullam extare, *temeritatem* enim autumant esse omnia.[1]

This characteristic of Fortuna is also strongly suggested by her earliest worship in Latium. The most ancient seats of her cult were at Praeneste and Antium, and here what little we know about her points to a deity or *numen* controlling men's fortunes, rather than one who simply represents luck good or bad. In each of these cities there was an *oraculum Fortunae*; and oracles, however simple and primitive,

[1] Ap. Auct. ad Herenn. ii. 23. The text is uncertain: see the edition of F. Marx, p. 240.

COSMIC IDEAS OF DEITY

were never associated with the idea of blind chance, but were supposed to be the voice of some power in the secrets of a destiny inscrutable by human devices.[1] The uncertain or unknown element in life was *fors*; Fortuna was the deity concerned with *fors*, and therefore capable of foretelling the future.

Of the oracle at Praeneste we have some knowledge —enough to put it beyond doubt that Fortuna was thought of as a power controlling the changes and chances of human life. Her cult-title here was *primigenia*, which can only mean first-born;[2] and an early inscription proves that it was Jupiter whose first-born she was. A woman gives an offering to her, " diovo filei primigenia," for help in childbirth (*nationu cratia*)[3]; she had no doubt consulted the oracle, which here as elsewhere in Italy foretold the future by means of *sortes*, mixed together by a boy before he drew one. True, this idea of a deity as the child of another is foreign to the old religions of Italy, so far as we know, and we must ascribe it in this instance to the invasion of Praeneste by Graeco-Etruscan ideas at an early period, a fact proved by excavations there. Probably the Latin deity had taken on some of the characteristics of the Greek

---

[1] See Bouché-Leclercq, *Hist. de la divination*, vol. i. ch. ii. "No man can escape his appointed fate," was the answer of the Delphic oracle to Croesus (Herod. i. 91).

[2] I have lately examined the evidence afresh, and can affix no other meaning to the word here. Primigenius always seems to mean the first or original item in a series: *e.g. primigenius sulcus* is the first sod cut in a new settlement, *i.e.* that which began the tracing of the city-boundary.

[3] See *Roman Festivals*, p. 224.

Tyche or Nemesis, and had thus come within the range of the cult of the heaven-god; but it is most unlikely that the mystery will ever be solved. One thing we can be sure of—that Jupiter is of all old Italian deities the one who can under no circumstances be associated with the idea of blind chance; and we may conclude that of Fortuna, his first-born daughter (if such she was), the same can be said. She must rather have been a power believed capable of governing the destiny of women in childbirth, possibly also that of the children to be born. She was at all times, and in many places besides Praeneste, especially a woman's deity; one to whom appeal might be made for help in trouble, more especially in the anxious time of childbirth.[1] There may have been other sides to her cult in Latium, but this is the one which is beyond doubt.

When she made her way to Rome, apparently from Etruria, towards the end of the regal period, it was not as the eldest born of Jupiter, nor in any cosmic sense, still less as a goddess of luck or chance; but in course of time, specialised and localised under various titles, she came to express the hopes of Roman men and women—especially the latter—in relation to particular activities or critical moments. The cult of Fors Fortuna, a reduplicate title quite in the Roman manner, was for example probably connected with the harvest; the dedication day of the temple was June 24, when much of the work of harvesting would be

---

[1] Wissowa, *R.K.* ed. 2, p. 256 foll.

COSMIC IDEAS OF DEITY

completed.[1] As Fortuna muliebris, also as Fortuna virilis, she was more especially a women's deity; and later on such titles as Fortuna equestris, Fortuna huiusce diei, and others, tell their own story clearly enough when we take the trouble to examine the circumstances of their origin. At the end of the Hannibalic war the great Fortuna of Praeneste was honoured with a temple in Rome, probably after successful recourse to her oracle, which so far the Roman authorities had declined to consult. But transplanted cults are apt to lose something of their original character, and here we find no first-born daughter of Jupiter, but rather the beginning of Fortuna publica Populi Romani, of which we hear so much later on.

I have thus briefly sketched the history of Fortuna as a Latin and Roman deity, because I wished to make it clear that there is nothing to suggest that the virile and persistent Roman ever believed himself or his State to be at the mercy of mere chance. I do not think that he ever thought of his deities of family or State as capricious; they were always open to supplication, and were practically bound to give way to it if approached by precisely the right methods. His *virtus*, his manly independence, never suffered from any sense of a capricious or irresistible power controlling him and his. We have unmistakable traces of this *virtus* in the earliest Roman literature; for example, one of the *sententiae* of the famous Appius Claudius Caecus (*circa* 300 B.C.) is the well-

---

[1] Cp. Columella x. 311 foll.; *Roman Festivals*, p. 170.

known saying, "Est unus quisque faber ipse fortunae suae,"[1] where we have *fortuna* already taking on the meaning of a man's condition or wealth, which has come down to us of to-day; and in the *Annals of Ennius*[2] we find the perennial proverb, "fortibus est fortuna viris data." In Plautus and Terence the influence of the Greek τύχη begins to appear, and the word begins to gain the ordinary meaning of luck which *fors* had originally expressed. But it is curious that in the only complete prose work of the period following the war with Hannibal, that of Cato on agriculture, Fortuna is not once mentioned. That war, which tried the nerve of the people so severely, was not likely to weaken their sense of the need of strenuous human endeavour. In spite of an attempt to introduce Epicurism early in that century, the better minds at Rome kept clear of any degrading doctrine of capricious chance, with its corollaries of individual selfishness and *laissez-faire*. And such doctrine was far indeed from being associated with the idea or worship of a deity.

This belief in *virtus*, in human endeavour, was upheld and confirmed by the presence and influence at Rome of those two remarkable Greeks, sympathetic

---

[1] The saying is quoted by the author of the *Epistola ad Caesarem de Republica*, i. 1. 2, and put into metre by Baehrens, *Fragm. Poet. Rom.* p. 36. It is worth noting that Fortuna is often conjoined with Spes (Roscher, *Lex.* s.v. "Spes") and with Fides, as in Hor. *Od.* i. 35. The Romans seem from the earliest times to have believed rather in character than fortune as the supreme good; "virtus" can counteract "fortuna." Cp. Gwatkin, *Knowledge of God*, i. p. 138.

[2] Baehrens, *Fragm. Poet. Rom.* p. 83.

admirers of the true Roman spirit, Panaetius the Stoic philosopher, and Polybius the philosophic historian. Greeks though they were, they form a part of the history of Roman thought. In each we find the freedom of the will asserted, and Man's dependence on his own active endeavour fully emphasised. Luckily we have Panaetius's opinion, or rather conviction, reproduced by Cicero in his *de Officiis*. Man is able by his own will and reason to work out his own fortune, in spite of the undoubted fact that chance has power to hinder as well as help him. "Magnam vim esse in fortuna in utramque partem, vel secundas ad res vel adversas, quis ignorat?"[1] But man must not sit down patiently to take whatever Fortune brings him; he must use his reason and his will in modifying for his own benefit and that of his fellow-men the conditions under which he lives. We need not be astonished that Panaetius, with this common-sense view of human life, rejected all kinds of divination, thus breaking with the older Stoic doctrine, and with the traditional Roman practice; for the more the philosopher exalts the position of man in nature, the less need will he ascribe to him of such devices for securing his interests in the future.

But what did Panaetius really mean by *fortuna*? This is not explained by Cicero; but we may be sure that he did not mean either a deity, or Fate, or any such abstraction. A rational philosopher, writing a

[1] *de Officiis*, ii. 6. 19; H. N. Fowler, *Panaetii Fragmenta*, 33.

plain treatise of ethics for practical Romans, is here probably using the word τύχη simply for the incalculable in human life, without reference to metaphysics. If you look at the comment which Aulus Gellius (xiii. 28) wrote upon this view of Panaetius, you will hardly doubt that by "fortunae verbera" he meant no more than the changes and chances of this mortal life.[1]

From Polybius we learn much more of the views of the thinking men of this age about Fortuna or τύχη. He was not a professed philosopher, but his mind was in some sense a philosophic one, and it is extremely interesting to note the use of Fortuna in his treatment of history. It is quite clear that he does not look upon her as a deity either Greek or Roman. In what remains of his work there is no allusion to the local Fortuna-cults of Rome and Italy, though within his own time three temples were dedicated to the goddess at Rome, one of them by the father of his intimate friend Scipio Aemilianus. Nor does he mention the numerous city Tychae of the Hellenistic age. This is characteristic of a man whose ideas of history and religion were cosmopolitan, and who did not greatly interest himself in the local cults of the City-states of his day. I may therefore seem to be wasting time in touching here on his views. But this is not so; for if he does not make Fortuna a deity, he does in several passages come very near to

---

[1] "The slings and arrows of outrageous fortune." The common idea of chance is nowhere better illustrated than in this soliloquy of Hamlet.

using the word τύχη as a divine agency of some vague kind, thus most fortunately illustrating the trend of thought which brought her into such prominence in the following century.

For example, in a remarkable fragment about the degeneracy and depopulation of Greece (xxxvii. 9), he writes as if he were himself almost willing to attribute them to Fortune or the gods. "As it is impossible, or at least difficult, to determine the causes of these events, it might be natural enough to ascribe them to God (ὁ Θεός) and to Fortune,"—where the two are scarcely distinguished.[1] Again in the famous chapter about Philip of Macedon (xxiii. 10) τύχη comes very near to being personified as a goddess, and as capable of inflicting punishment like the Nemesis of Greek tragedy, which Polybius seems to have been thinking of when he wrote this chapter in a more emotional vein than was usual with him.[2] So too at the very end of his history, when bidding his reader farewell (xxxix. 10) he writes of τύχη as a power having influence on men's lives, not capriciously, but in the regular order of things—a cosmic power or process, like the φύσις of his sixth book (e.g. vi. 9. 10), which itself in many passages seems to be almost equivalent to his use of τύχη, for each of them suggests the idea of an agent or power working to a definite end.[3] We must not, of course, forget that τύχη had been used in this sense from Aristotle downwards, i.e. to express

---

[1] Polyb. xxxvii. 9.   [2] *Ibid.* xxiii. 10.
[3] *Ibid.* xxxix. 19; cp. vi. 9. 10. See *Classical Review*, vol. xvii. 445. foll.

what happens in the natural order of things, without any ascription to it of wantonness or caprice, and beyond doubt including in its operation the agency of Man, whose will is free. Man is subject, no doubt, to the "economy of nature" (vi. 9), but he is himself an important factor in it. This power is very close to the Stoic εἱμαρμένη;[1] it was used by writers like Polybius very much as "evolution" is often used by modern historians, to express the natural course of events, without any very definite or technical meaning. But in the language of Stoics this evolutionary process might also, without inconsistency, be called God.

Not indeed the god of conventional language, which must not be taken as reflecting any philosophical or theological views of Polybius or any other writer. Writers at this time, and for long afterwards, use *deus* or θεός where sudden chances, providential escapes and so on are described, which cannot well be accounted for scientifically; and this may well be at the root of that popularity of a degraded form of Fortuna to which I am coming directly. This was a time when thinking men had dropped their polytheism, and yet were far from clear about any divine agency that might take its place. The vagueness of their ideas is reflected in the diversity of terms they use—they are as it were searching after scientific truth, like Polybius, and are yet very far from even approaching it. Neither in terms of religion nor philosophy are they able to express those vague ideas

[1] Cic. *Div.* i. 55-125.

adequately, yet they are ready to use the first of either of the two categories that happens to come uppermost.

Whether Polybius himself believed in a divine government of the world is hard to say; but it is certain that he did not trouble himself about it where he could dispense with it in his expositions. Listen to his own words: "Those things of which it is impossible to ascertain the causes ... may reasonably be ascribed to God or Fortune, if no cause can easily be discovered. On such matters we may naturally follow the opinions of the multitude for lack of exact knowledge, and by prayers and sacrifices and oracles try to ascertain what we can do to better our condition. But where it is possible to discover the causes, remote and immediate, of the event in question, I do not think that in such cases we ought to have recourse to divine agency in order to explain them."[1] Thus for men like Polybius the sphere of divine interposition would be continually diminishing; and they are not too ready to find a name for the agent who is narrowing that sphere.

I pass on to the great intellects of the last century B.C. Taking Cicero first, it is not easy to gain a clear impression of his idea of Fortuna; he was not a man of strong convictions, and wrote in many varying moods. In his later years he was strongly drawn towards Stoicism, and in the passage from his *de Officiis* which I quoted just now he approves the

[1] Polybius xxxvii. 9. 2.

opinion of Panaetius that Fortuna is a power working for good or evil on man, but that man can counteract her by his own will in most matters of real importance. But Cicero, under the influence of the terrible uncertainty of social and political life in his age, felt beyond doubt the stern reality of Fortuna, good and bad, more keenly than would have been approved by Panaetius. The Fortuna of his ordinary moods is not the old Latin deity, but the later Greek Tyche; she is *volubilis, inconstans, caeca,* and so on, and it is in his writings that we first meet with mention of her wheel (*rota*).[1] This may indeed be little more than conventional literary language, expressing no very definite conviction; but it reflects the popular opinion of the age, and it is Cicero's when he is not philosophising. For his more serious conviction let us turn to the *de Divinatione,* written almost at the end of a life chequered by many turns of Fortune's wheel (44 B.C.). We shall find it much the same. In the first book of this work his brother Quintus is supposed

[1] An examination of Cicero's views leads me to the following conclusions: (1) Practically he feels the influence of his time, and his own experience has taught him that Fortuna is a reality. Cp. among many other passages, *Nat. Deor.* ii. 43; *de Amicit.* 103; (2) He is clear that Man can resist Fortuna and get the better of her; *Parad. Stoi.* 5; *Tusc.* v. 2. 3, cp. 25 and 26; *Off.* ii. 19, 20; *Pro Marcell.* 7. (3) In his last works he writes more philosophically, e.g. *Div.* ii. 15 foll., where it is plain that he is uncomfortable with the Stoic Fate, and feels too strongly the force of his own free will and the sport of Chance in the history of his time. But he will not accept either Fate alone or Chance alone. Perhaps the most useful passage is in *Acad. Priora,* vii. 29, where he says that the same universal force is called by some "prudentia," by some "necessitas," by others "fortuna,"—the last because they do not understand the causation in the particular case. See Reid's valuable notes *ad loc.*

to state the Stoic view as represented by Posidonius, who differed from his master Panaetius in maintaining that Man can to some extent unravel the mystery of the future, of fate, the " ex omni aeternitate fluens veritas sempiterna " of the Stoics. In the second book Cicero himself (though an augur) argues against this position, and here we seem to find his own view of Fortuna. Divination, he says, whether of predetermined fate or things accidental, is altogether impossible. " Quomodo ergo id quod temere fit caeco casu et volubilitate fortunae, praesentiri et praedici potest ? "[1] Fortune beyond doubt exists, he argues, and is contrary to reason and *constantia* ; and not even a god can foreknow what is going to happen *casu et fortuito*. So too in the *de Fato*, written soon after the *de Divinatione*, he asserts that Fate is the product of the brain of philosophers ; common sense and experience teach us that *natura* and *fortuna* both exist, but not inevitable Fate.[2] " Where is the need to foist in fate, when the universe can be explained by reference to *natura* and *fortuna* ? " We may agree that Cicero has not really thought out the problem, and is not too clear as to the meaning he attaches to *fatum, fortuna, natura* ; but his words are

[1] *de Div.* ii. 15 *fin.*, and 18.
[2] *de Fato*, iii. 6 foll. Natura and Fortuna are distinguished in *de Amic.* 103 : " Equidem ex omnibus rebus quas mihi aut natura aut fortuna tribuit . . . " where the contrast is between a man's own contribution to his life, and that of external circumstances. But in this passage of the *de Fato* they seem almost identical (whether *que* be read or *ve*). The view he expresses is no doubt that of Posidonius, and has come down to him from earlier Stoics.

valuable because they are based on his own personal experience of life, and reflect no doubt the experience of many of his contemporaries. He has too lively a sense of his own free will, to believe in sheer necessity; indeed his intense humanity forbade it.[1]

The passage is also interesting, because it seems almost to identify Natura and Fortuna, as Polybius seems almost to identify τύχη and φύσις; and we must not forget that Lucretius used *fortuna gubernans* to mean the same thing as *natura gubernans*. In v. 77 he wrote :

> praeterea solis cursus lunaeque meatus
> expediam qua vi flectat natura gubernans :

and only a few lines later he speaks of *fortuna gubernans* in exactly the same sense, for the power, whatever it be, that thus steers the universe. On these lines Munro notes that the Epicurean " Nature " is at one and the same time blind chance and inexorable necessity, comparing vi. 31, " seu casu seu vi, quod sic natura parasset."

But neither Cicero nor Lucretius thought of this power as a deity, though (as I hinted in the last lecture) they may both have had moments when they might think of it as in some sense divine. Nor did the other great intellect of that age, of whom it has often been said that he believed in his own luck or star as helping him through life. I endeavoured to show, I hope with success, in the *Classical Review* [2] that this cannot be proved from Caesar's own writings,

[1] *Acad. Prior.* vii. 29. [2] Vol. xvii. 153.

and that when he mentions Fortuna it is only in the ordinary sense of luck or accident, which might be counteracted by a man's own will and energy.

But if Caesar himself had no superstition about Fortuna, and never personified her, this was not so with his younger contemporaries. The experience of the last century of the Republic might well suggest a belief in the blind or wilful dominion of chance in human affairs; society and politics seemed to be governed by no benevolent destiny, nor any rational law of development. Cicero himself had spoken of Fortuna in this sense when pleading before Caesar for Marcellus, and leaves us in doubt whether we are to write the word with a capital F or no. A great general, he says, has many things to help him, but the greatest of all is Fortuna, who claims for her own credit all advantage that he gains; and immediately afterwards he calls her " rerum humanarum domina," though insisting that Caesar had no use for her, so great were his skill and foresight in warfare—" nunquam enim temeritas cum sapientia commiscetur, nec ad consilium casus admittitur." [1] Cicero is quite consistent here; he had always believed in Man's ability to counteract Fortuna; but only the most highly gifted can do this, and Caesar is so highly gifted, he adds, that he was rather to be compared with gods than men. The passage is for several

[1] *Pro Marcello*, 2. 7, " Quin etiam illa ipsa rerum humanarum domina, Fortuna, in istius se societatem gloriae non offert, tibi cedit, tuam esse totam et propriam fatetur. Nunquam enim temeritas cum sapientia commiscetur, nec ad consilium casus admittitur."

reasons an interesting one, and in my view forms an excellent proof of the genuineness of this speech.

But other writers of the same age, less thoughtful than Caesar and Cicero, seem to think of Fortuna as a wanton power that in those troubled times had found her opportunity, and was revelling in the contemplation of Man groping about in darkness, not knowing where he treads. Thus Sallust introduces her to us in this guise: "Sed profecto fortuna in omni re dominatur; ea res cunctas ex lubidine magis quam ex vero celebrat obscuratque."[1] A little further on (ch. x.), while looking on the progress of the Roman dominion as the result of *labor* and *iustitia* down to the destruction of Carthage, he declares that after that terrible event "saevire Fortuna ac miscere omnia coepit." The author of the book on the Alexandrian war speaks of Fortuna almost as a deity like the Greek Nemesis, reserving for a harder fate those on whom she has heaped benefits. And Cornelius Nepos (*Dion.* vi.) says that the fickleness of Fortuna began to sink the hero whom she had but just before exalted.

We must not indeed make too much of rhetorical expressions like these; they do not actually make Fortuna into a malicious deity, hardly even into a personal power revelling in the results of her own caprice. And they are not borne out by the literature of the Augustan age, in which the two finest spirits, Virgil and Livy, both serious men,

[1] *Catilina* 8, "Surely Fortuna holds supreme power in all things; she brings them to light or hides them away, acting rather by caprice than on principle." Cp. ch. 10.

intensely human, right-minded, never make any contribution to the idea of Fortuna as a capricious or cruel power. Virgil's Fortuna seems to me to be well expressed by Heinze:[1] "She is not so much a deity, as Reason and Providence conceived and expressed as the benevolent will of a deity," *i.e.* as the *numen*, favourable to the Roman state, of some great cosmic personality—of Jupiter in the Stoic plenitude of his sovereignty. To take a single striking example of this: after the burning of the ships, when the hero is minded to stay in Sicily, crushed by the blow, old Nautes thus addresses him:

> Nate dea, quo fata trahunt retrahuntque sequamur:
> Quicquid erit, superanda omnis fortuna ferendo est.[2]

Here, if the whole passage be read, it becomes clear (to me at least) that Fortuna is the will of the gods (or of God), against which a man can struggle if he will, but submission to which is really victory. She is a moral force, to which all men and states owe obedience and faith, inspired by that sense of duty to god and man which the Romans called *pietas*.

In Livy too we see the same tendency, not perhaps always successful, to make Fortuna into a moral force. For him she is the same vaguely conceived almighty power, not so much actually a deity, as a divine or heavenly power, *caeleste numen*,[3] working

[1] *Vergils epische Technik*, p. 287.   [2] *Aen.* v. 709.
[3] Livy i. 21 init. It seems clear that Livy had no doctrine of Fortuna; that he attributed success to human effort as well as good luck; but that he believed in something like Virgil's Destiny of the Roman people (*e.g.* i. 46, ii. 40, vi. 30). But in his most serious moments, as when he wrote his

behind the gods. But for more detail about Livy's Fortuna I must refer you to some excellent remarks in Weissenborn's preface to his edition, p. 19.

Time forbids me to pursue the history of Fortuna further here. I have sketched it for the period of the earlier empire in Hastings's *Dictionary of Religion and Ethics*, to which I will venture to refer you. I hope I may have shown in what I have just been saying that both among the thoughtful and the careless Romans of the last century of the Republic, the idea of Fortuna, in whatever sense understood, had become curiously prominent and excited a very unusual interest. I have been compelled to deal with her, because she seems so often to be on the very confines of divinity—a part or aspect of the Power manifesting itself in the universe. Under the Empire she was washed back again, so to speak, into the old sluggish current of State worships, both as Fortuna Populi Romani and as an important element in the worship of the Caesars; and in private worship she also appears as the mysterious Panthea, exalted as it would seem into a position in which she unites the attributes of all the other deities, and as Fortuna-Isis, perhaps as the result of an old connexion with seafaring, common to both deities.

But there is no doubt that the notion of Fortuna as a cosmic force survived into the imperial period, and even gained fresh force there, especially among

---

preface, Fortuna was not in his mind at all. There it is the Roman quality that has made Rome great, and the want of it that caused her decline.

the common people of no special culture, who have left their thousands of records on stone in every province as well as in Italy. Those records entirely bear out the famous passage of Pliny in which he says that "toto mundo et omnibus locis omnibusque horis omnium vocibus Fortuna sola invocatur et nominatur, una accusatur, una agitur rea, una cogitatur, sola laudatur, sola arguitur." [1] In the debit and credit of human accounts—adversity and prosperity—everything is set down to her. Pliny seems to think that mankind have found in her some causative agent who is not exactly a deity; "adeo obnoxiae sumus sortis, ut sors ipsa pro deo sit, qua deus probatur incertus." Like Polybius, he sees no harm in attributing events to a deity, or to Fortuna or *sors*, where no scientific account is to be had of them.

This most remarkable passage, with the whole context, I strongly advise you to study carefully. And when you have studied it, turn to the *Carmina Epigraphica* compiled by Buecheler, where even without the help of the index you will find abundant confirmation of Pliny. So many are the passages in which Fortuna occurs that the editor has failed to index them, simply writing, "Fortuna dea quadragies fere." Fortuna *dea*; but how often in these lines is she really thought of as a deity? It would be worth while to make a special study of this question with the help of the *Corpus*, as well as of the *Carmina*, where

[1] *Hist. Nat.* ii. 22.

in matters like this the cream of the *Corpus* is to be found. I suspect that she is as often as not a blind and reckless force, the worst companion a man can have to help him through life.

As proof of this, I may conclude this lecture with a few words from the well-known passage of Apuleius about initiation into the mysteries of Isis.[1] It seems to me to illustrate at once the chaos of common thought in the first century A.D., and the salvation that a youth might find in one of the "mystery religions," where he would land as on a solid rock after tossing on a perilous sea. When the young Lucius is initiated by the priest into the mysteries of the goddess, he is told that he has passed out of the capricious power of the blind and reckless Fortuna into the loving care of a Fortuna (*i.e.* Isis-Fortuna) who is not blind, and who even illuminates the other gods by her own light. "Behold, freed from his former troubles, rejoicing in the provident care of great Isis, Lucius triumphs over his own Fortune."[2]

---

[1] Apuleius xi. 15.

[2] I may add here an interesting passage about Fortuna dating from the very end of Paganism, in that short treatise or catechism of Sallustius which Professor G. Murray has translated at the end of his *Four Stages of Greek Religion*, chapter ix. p. 201 : "The power of the gods which orders for the good things which are not uniform, and which happen contrary to expectation, is commonly called Fortune, and it is for this reason that the goddess is especially worshipped in public by cities : for every city consists of elements which are not uniform. Fortune has power beneath the moon, since above the moon no single thing can happen by fortune. If Fortune makes a wicked man prosperous and a good man poor, there is no need to wonder. For the wicked regard wealth as everything, the good as nothing. And the good fortune of the bad cannot take away their badness, while virtue alone will be enough for the good."

LECTURE IV

THE RISE OF THE IDEA OF THE MAN-GOD

WE must now leave the heights where we have been contemplating Jupiter, the Sun, Fate, and Fortuna, and descend to look at the practical working of the ordinary Roman mind, which was really interested only in Man as a social being; mainly in Man as a Roman citizen, and in gods as inhabitants of Rome. By the Roman mind I mean to include Cicero in his ordinary moods, when he was not temporarily moved by emotion or by the study of Greek philosophers; and Varro, so far as we know him, at all times and in all moods. For them Man as a social being, and the Roman citizen in particular, was, if not the measure of the universe, at any rate more important than all the rest of it. The lofty doctrines of the Soul of the world or the universal Reason did, of course, interest men like these two; but they could not be satisfied unless the World-soul could be brought into immediate relation to the Roman State and its deities, and such a process was hardly possible, even through the agency of Jupiter. Let me illustrate this characteristic of the Roman mind for a moment; it is of the utmost importance for my subject in this lecture.

Varro, so far as we can guess from the fragments of his work on the Roman religious antiquities, seems to have persuaded himself of the truth of the Stoic doctrine of the *anima mundi*, and to have tried to reconcile it with his own feeling about the deities and cults of the Roman state—a feeling genuinely Roman or Italian. That feeling is not easy for us to understand, but it must be understood if we are to get any real insight into the religious chaos of an age when even at Rome, where we should never have expected it, the old cults of the State were wearing out. Varro tells us frankly enough that the gods of the State are simply human institutions. Take for example the 4th fragment in Agahd's collection,[1] where he says that he wrote of human antiquities before treating of the divine ones, " quia divinae istae ab hominibus institutae sunt." This no doubt refers rather to the various cults, which had in fact been instituted by the State; but it implies, in characteristic Roman fashion, that the gods would have been nothing to the Romans if the State had not established their worship. Nay, he can go a step further and say that the very existence of the gods depends on that worship —a view in one sense profoundly true at Rome, as elsewhere in the pagan world. In another passage, quoted by St. Augustine, he expresses a fear lest some

[1] ap. Aug. *Civ. Dei*, vi. 4 (Agahd, p. 143).

of them should perish simply from neglect (*civium neglegentia*).[1] How well this proves the truth of the maxim that the study of the Roman religion begins and ends with the cult, and how well it explains the absence of myths at Rome, and the wasted labour of those who treat Graeco-Roman mythology as if it were genuine Italian! But from this sad fate Varro is trying to save the gods by this very treatise of his —from *ignobilitas*, as he expressively calls it.[2] He feared, he says, that some had already suffered *ignobilitas*, and were beyond restoration.

Cicero, though he does not speak quite so plainly, so uncompromisingly, does none the less make it clear that he holds the same opinion of the gods of the State. If we look at the introduction to the *de Natura Deorum*, we shall find what seem to be his own views, perhaps convictions, about those gods. "Gods," he says, "are needed for the maintenance of the social system; without them society would be a chaos (*magna confusio*); *fides, iustitia, societas generis humani* would all go to pieces."[3] The gods must exist because they have this definite function of holding the State together; therein is their only *raison d'être*. As an argument for the existence of gods, this does not come to much; it only proved that Man had invented or discovered something which had turned out well and been of value to him—something which he ought to preserve carefully, lest (as

---

[1] Aug. *C.D.* vi. 2 (Agahd, p. 141).   [2] *Ib.* (Agahd, p. 142).
[3] Cic. *N.D.* i. 2. 3.

Varro said) it should decay and disappear in a melancholy *ignobilitas*.

Both Varro and Cicero then are true Italians in their way of looking at this question; they think of the gods as the divine inhabitants of the City-state, maintaining its life and protecting its armies, and except in regard to these functions, as being without interest for the human inhabitants. Even when their thoughts rise for a moment from the State to the universe, from practical life to Stoic philosophy, they think of the universe and its deity in terms of the State and of human society. This at any rate is true of Cicero, who hated the Epicureans just because their gods had no interest in human affairs, and possessed none of that active force to which the true Roman ascribed the maintenance of his State morally and physically. But the Stoic doctrine of the divine origin of human law and society he revered, and in his writings we have more than one fine and clear statement of it. In the Laws, for example, the universe is pictured as a great *civitas* or constitution, under the government of an almighty deity, who holds together all the grades of human association.[1]

Thus, whether they contemplate the old gods of the State or the new idea of the one great Power or deity pervading the universe, they cannot get free

---

[1] *de Legibus*, i. 23, "... ut iam universus hic mundus una civitas sit communis deorum atque hominum existimanda. Et quod in civitatibus ratione quadam ... agnationibus familiarum distinguuntur status, id in rerum natura tanto est magnificentius tantoque praeclarius, ut homines deorum agnatione et gente teneantur." Cp. *de Rep.* iii. 22.

of the influence of the State and society. If there is to be any form of deity at Rome, apart from the gods of the simplest type of social life in the family, it must be in close relation with the State and its government, in immediate relation to man and the needs of his daily life. When Cicero is speaking of the binding force of the oath in social and political life, he explains it as the result of the fact that the immortal gods are present acting both as *testes* and *iudices*.[1] But if those "immortal" gods—the adjective was by this time a conventional one—should become obsolete, *ignobiles*, perishing through the neglect of the citizens, what was to take their place in such matters as this of the oath? Who was to look after the needs of the citizen, moral and physical? The lofty Pantheism of the Stoics, try as they might, could not take the place of the gods of the State; there was no real compromise to be found between the World-soul and these gods, even if you treated them as emanations of that one great principle, as both Cicero and Varro tried to do.[2] Philosophic deism, monotheism in the form of Jupiter or the Sun, would appeal to the educated only, and they would inevitably grow more and more contemptuous of the popular beliefs and prejudices, as in another lecture I shall show that they did at Rome. On the other hand, the uneducated, the foreigners, and the freedmen, who now made up such a large part of the Roman popula-

[1] *de Legibus*, ii. 7. 16.
[2] See my *Social Life at Rome in the Age of Cicero*, p. 336.

tion, were naturally callous about the old city cults, and prone to surrender themselves to new ones like that of Isis, or to live without gods at all, abandoning *religio* for *superstitio*.

Yet it was possible to find a religion (if we may use the word) in close relation with the government and institutions of the State, and one which, skilfully used, need not interfere either with the doctrine of the World-soul as deity or even with the worship of the old deities of the State ; one too that would not need much finding, but was ready to hand, suggested by the circumstances of the time. The exaltation of a powerful human being into a god or a " superman " was, it is true, quite unprecedented in Rome and Italy, as I will show directly—the idea was an exotic one. But if the seed were brought to Italy, the condition of the Italian soil was at that moment favourable to its germination. In that age of ill-used capitalism and unsparing cruelty, of fraud and injustice in private and public life, what aid were the old deities giving to their people ? For long past, all over the Mediterranean world, it had been proved that Man was more helpful than god, and it was natural enough that a man, if he made the conditions of this life more bearable, should be looked on as something more than human. Where men were ceasing everywhere to put their trust in the worship of gods in whose power to help they did not any longer really believe, where therefore " the old forms of worship were emptied of their real significance, there was less hesitation in offering them to men."[1] It is most interesting to notice that Cicero himself had almost unconsciously suggested this solution of the problem in his *Dream of Scipio*, which ended his treatise on government. His practical Roman instinct, needing a direct relation between the State and deity, seems to hint to him that the great and good man placed in a position to control a State, the *moderator reipublicae* of his work on the State, might reasonably be thought of as something more than human in the ordinary Roman sense : at least that after his death he should ascend to the abode of the gods. " Bene meritis de patria quasi limes ad caeli aditum patet " (26). The great rulers of mankind are heaven-born, and to heaven return (13).

We are gradually shedding that old delusion, in which I was historically brought up, that there must necessarily be something vulgar or degrading in the worship of a man, one of these rulers, whether alive or dead. It has indeed taken us a long time to cultivate a historical sense in thinking of this. As college tutor I used to the last to rejoice in Tiberius's noble speech in the Senate, refusing to allow temples to be erected to him in Spain—" ego, patres conscripti, me mortalem esse vos testor "[2]—as an oasis in a dreary desert of flattery and self-humiliation, and used to point out with scorn the mean sneer of Tacitus at what seemed to him such imbecility in the

---

[1] These words are those of Mr. Bevan in Hastings's *Dictionary of Religion and Ethics*, vol. iv. 525.   [2] Tac. *Ann.* iv. 38.

Emperor. I believe that I should feel and say just the same now if I had to talk about that surprising passage, so clear is its unintended comment on the much-maligned character of an honest man. But I can see now that in spite of the miserable failure of Tacitus to point the right moral, he is probably representing more exactly than I used to think, the real feeling of the Spanish petitioners for the privilege of worshipping the emperor. Or to take another example from the same reign, when Velleius tells us that Tiberius " sacravit parentem suum non imperio sed religione, non appellavit eum sed fecit deum," [1] I do not doubt that the soldier-historian was quite in earnest, and from the point of view of his time justly so ; the deification of the dead Augustus was not a merely official or political act, but a genuine confession of devotion towards one who had wrought great things for the world and proclaimed a gospel of peace and glad tidings.

It only needs a little reflection to see how near this comes to the language of Lucretius about Epicurus, which no one would pick out for condemnation,[2] " deus ille fuit, deus, inclute Memmi," —who found out wisdom, and by his skill rescued life from storm and darkness, and moored it in a calm anchorage under a bright light. Of Empedocles, who had indeed himself claimed to be a god,[3]

---

[1] Vell. Pat. ii. 126.   [2] Bk. v. *init.*

[3] Diog. Laert. viii. 59 foll. Lucretius i. 726 foll. " The poems of his godlike genius cry with trumpet-voice, and set forth his glorious discoveries in such wise, that he seems scarce born of mortal stock " (J. M.).

THE IDEA OF THE MAN-GOD

he speaks almost as strongly, but with just a shade of hesitation :

> Carmina quin etiam divini pectoris eius
> Vociferantur et exponunt praeclara reperta,
> Ut vix humana videatur stirpe creatus.

In the same spirit Plato had, of course, been called a god; Cicero for example, in the second book of the *Nat. Deor.*, speaks of him as "quasi quendam deum philosophorum," as Panaetius had done before him,[1] if we may believe Galen. No doubt this was a way of speaking, not to be taken too literally, as we may guess from other passages of Cicero, *e.g.* in the *de Oratore*, bk. i., where Scaevola calls Antonius "deum in dicendo;"[2] but just as with St. Paul's mystery language, which by no means proves that he believed in Greek mysteries, the use of the word *deus* in this sense by a sensible practical Roman shows the nature of the ideas in the air at the time.[3] The use of the adjective *divinus* points in the same direction; Cicero thought of Aristotle as having an "ingenium paene divinum," and of Sophocles as "poeta divinus."[4] In the first book of *de Divinatione* the word is used in a peculiar sense to mean "capable of foreseeing the future," *i.e.* possessed of superhuman power; the soul, for example, is "multo divinior" (more inspired) at the approach of death.[5] Thus the astrologer might

---

[1] *N.D.* ii. 32, with Mayor's note ; *Tusc.* i. 39.
[2] *de Oratore*, i. 106.   [3] Cp. Cic. *pro Marcello*, 3. 8 *ad fin.*
[4] *Div.* i. 53. Cp. Dr. A. C. Bradley (*Shakespearean Tragedy*, p. 287), "This is one of those passages that make one worship Shakespeare."
[5] *Div.* i. 28, 58 and 59.

be counted as of superhuman rank, as Cumont shows in his book on astrology and religion (p. 148).

There was then clearly a floating suspicion even at Rome that there is in Man a possibility of something over and above our common human nature, something that Greeks could express by the word δαίμων, Romans by *genius*—the latter a very convenient word, as it turned out, when the floating idea had to be utilised for a definite and practical purpose, as in modern times, too, when men wish to express mysterious powers of feeling and intellect which they cannot fully explain or understand. Philosophers were moved by the same feeling when they preached the doctrine of the divinity of the soul. The old Orphic and Pythagorean idea that the soul is a divine thing imprisoned in the body, which the earlier Stoics could not accept, was revived in a modified form by the later Stoics and especially by Posidonius, and is expressed plainly by Cicero in several passages. In the *Republic* he had said of Man that with all his faults he had within him " quidam divinus ignis ingenii et mentis." [1] In his writings of the last years of his life the same idea is often expressed.[2] Our best word for this " vis divina mentis " is perhaps *inspiration*, which has been used of late for religious insight as well as for poetical impulse. " In the depths of some individual consciousness, amid the actions and

---

[1] *Rep.* iii. 1 (Aug. *contra Pelagium*, iv. 12); cp. *Somn. Scip.* ch. xxiv., " Deum te igitur scito esse," etc.; *Roman Religious Experience*, p. 368 foll.
[2] *Tusc.* i. 65 and 70; *N.D.* i. 1 and passages cited by Mayor in his note.

counteractions of the human and the divine, a sacred fire is kindled, a purpose is born." These words of Professor Gardner [1] will apply equally well to our notion of the inspiration of the poet and the prophet; it is the idea at the root of Carlyle's *Hero Worship*; it is made to explain men of will and power to govern, as well as men of thought and feeling. How near it comes to the idea of the divinity of the soul we may see if we reflect that Man, already above all other creatures, if he is to rise any higher, *must* tend to become God—that at least is the only way in which we can express it. We are reminded of the Stoic argument for the existence of God from the scale of existence, originally suggested by Aristotle.[2] Man strives, or should strive, to make his way up to God, having within him a spark of divinity already, according to the Stoic view of his participation in Reason, which is in perfection in God only.

Such were some of the ideas floating in Graeco-Italian air in the last two centuries B.C. It has been necessary for me to touch on them, in order to show that the trend of thought at that time was not wholly inconsistent with man-worship. But such ideas had to contend with the whole force of Roman and Italian religious tradition, which at no point, unless it be in the conception of Genius, seems to admit the near approach of Man to Deity. I must now turn for a few minutes to this aspect of the subject; for

---

[1] *Historic View of the New Testament*, p. 46.
[2] See Mayor's note on *N.D.* ii. 33.

it has often been maintained that precedents for Caesar-worship could be found in Italy.

If my interpretation of the Roman religion is the right one, the deification of Man was not a natural process of the Roman mind. The Roman deities were not personal ones, but functional forces of nature, with a tendency to form abstractions; and thus they were much further removed from men than those of Greece or Egypt. Dr. Frazer has indeed attempted to show that Roman kings might personate gods, and that gods married (*mated* is his favourite word) and had children like men.[1] If this were so, it would bring the Romans within easy reach of apotheosis; but the literary evidence is worthless for the true Roman way of thinking, being entirely Greek and not earlier than the third century B.C. The personation of Jupiter by the triumphator is, like the architecture and ritual of the great temple on the Capitol, Graeco-Etruscan, and dates from the period when Rome was in the hands of Etruscan conquerors. We must, of course, in investigating the rise of apotheosis in Italy, reckon duly with Greek and Etruscan influence, and also with that of the East and Egypt, for these had by the time of Cicero all become formative components of the Roman religious consciousness. But at the same time we must bear in mind the essential features of true

---

[1] *Lectures on the Early History of Kingship*, p. 204 foll. Professor G. Murray has recently adopted this idea from Frazer (*Rise of the Greek Epic*, ed. 2, p. 160), which I tried to refute in *R. R. Exp.* p. 51.

native Italian religion, as we are certain that Augustus and his successor did when they had to deal with this delicate problem.

Let us ask, then, in the first place, whether the Roman religion shows any trace of intermediaries between man and god, or anything to suggest the idea of a germ of divinity in man? We may dismiss at once the Greek hero, who never had much weight outside his own country; when Hercules and the Twin Brethren came to Rome, they came as full-blown gods, and Cicero classes them with Quirinus and the deities of abstractions.[1] He distinguishes them, it is true, from those who have always been reckoned *caelestes*, and speaks of them as having gained heaven on their merits, but none the less for the Romans they were always gods, not heroes. Of demigods in Italy (to use the old expression) we can be sure of none, though there may be a possibility that Faunus and Silvanus, as H. Nettleship suggested long ago, represent an ancient people of the mountain and woodland, such as the Veddahs of Ceylon. This view I adopted with some modification in *Roman Festivals* (p. 263) in treating of Faunus, quoting

---

[1] *de Legibus*, ii. 19. "Quirinus" here seems to mean "Romulus." But the connexion between the god and Romulus is late, not before 54 B.C. or thereabouts. See Wissowa, *R.K.* ed. 2, p. 155 note. Hence we may infer that the deification of Romulus was late also. Dr. Frazer treats it as a primitive fact in *G.B.*, ed. 2, vol. ii. p. 182, but his evidence proves nothing. Livy i. 16 is romance, and not meant to be anything else. The story in *de Legibus*, i. 3, betrays its romantic character at once; Proculus Julius, walking in his garden, had an interview with the deceased Romulus, who stated that he was a god.

Tylor and Sir A. Lyall for the attribution of supernatural powers to wild men of the hills and woods,[1] and noting the complete absence of votive inscriptions in honour of this deity. But I am not sure that this theory is the right one, and if it were, it would have little bearing on the question before us. Faunus did not belong to city life, where alone apotheosis could arise; if it was Faunus who played the chief part in the Lupercalia, which I do not myself believe, his meaning was entirely lost at a very early period. Silvanus was far more distinctly a real god; and I know of no other figure which could be reckoned as intermediary between god and man. Varro, when speaking of demigods, can mention no other example than Faunus,[2] and Faunus does not carry us very far.

Next, was there at Rome a connecting link between the human and the divine in the form of a belief in the divine descent of high families? The answer to this seems to be that there is no evidence of an early Roman belief in the divine descent of either gens or family. To appreciate this fact, a student may be advised to read side by side the articles in the *Dictionary of Antiquities* on *gens* and γένος, both by an excellent authority, the late Dr. Greenidge. What was a common belief in Hellas is not to be found at

---

[1] Since then the same suggestion has been put forward to account for Pheres or Centaurs of Greece by Professor Ridgway, *Early Age of Greece*, vol. i. p. 173 foll. Cp. Lawson, *Modern Greek Folk-lore and Ancient Greek Religion*, p. 244.

[2] Serv. Interpol. *Aen.* viii. 275 (Agahd, p. 153).

IV THE IDEA OF THE MAN-GOD

Rome in a genuine Italian form. Some Roman *gentes* traced their descent up to Alba Longa, or had special religious rites to look after (as the Julii those of Veiovis at Bovillae), but as we might expect, what interested the Roman here as elsewhere was practical duty, not mythological fancy. He never reached the idea of divine descent until he learnt it from the Greeks. For example, the descent from Venus claimed by the Julii in Caesar's time [1] was the result of the arrival of Venus Erycina after the First Punic War, with the Aeneas legend in her train. When the idea was once started it soon gained ground, and undoubtedly became of use in the hands of Julius and Augustus. Cicero seems to have had an inkling of the idea, but no more; "antiquitas," he says, "proxime accedit ad deos"; but the context shows that he understands this in a Roman spirit, viz. that the religious duties of the family are a charge given

---

[1] Wissowa, *R.K.* ed. 2, p. 292. The divine descent of Romulus has already been touched on. The earliest mention of it is in Ennius, *Annals*, ii. fragm. 73 Baehrens :

O Romule Romule die
Qualem te patriae custodem di genuerunt.
O pater, o genitor, o sanguen dis oriundum.

This is probably a reminiscence of the Greek idea of the divinity of legendary founders of cities : see Bevan in Hastings's *Dictionary of Religion and Ethics*, vol. iv. p. 525*a*, at bottom. Whether Italian legends of founders, which were numerous, also suggest that the idea was indigenous there, is a difficult question. Dr. Frazer thinks so; see *G.B.* ed. 3, vol. ii. ch. xiv. I take this opportunity of pointing out the worthlessness of the evidence on which some of these stories rest; *e.g.* what Dr. Frazer calls, following Plutarch, Promathion's *History of Italy* (*vita Romuli*, 2 ad fin.). Except in this passage this ἱστορία Ἰταλική is never heard of, and the name of the writer is itself suspicious. I am disposed to think that it was a romance of the type common in the Hellenistic age.

it by the gods.[1] Varro in an interesting fragment mentions the belief, but most characteristically gives it a practical turn. "It is useful in a State," he says, "that *viri fortes* should believe themselves to be descended from the gods, for it stimulates the human mind to strenuous endeavour and vigorous action."[2] *Noblesse oblige*. Doubtless he had in his mind the divine descent of Julius, to whom as pontifex maximus he dedicated the book containing this passage. But his dictum is one of general application, and reminds us of Dr. Frazer's first proposition in his *Psyche's Task*,[3] that superstition has strengthened the respect for government, especially that of kings, and thereby contributed to the maintenance of civil order; a dictum which Polybius had already applied to the Roman aristocracy.

Closely connected with the idea of divine descent is that of the divinity of the king or chief, now so familiar to us from the labours of Dr. Frazer. The king is not only divine by virtue of his descent, but is in possession of divine powers—magical powers which are not of human origin. This of course was well known in the Orient, and must have greatly aided Alexander and his successors in their claims to divinity, and through them contributed, as we shall

---

[1] *de Legibus*, ii. 27, "Iam ritus familiae patrumque servare id est (quoniam antiquitas proxime accedit ad deos) a dis quasi traditam religionem tueri."

[2] Aug. *Civ. Dei*, iii. 4 (Agahd, p. 154).

[3] *Psyche's Task*, p. 4 foll. (cp. Polybius vi. 54). On p. 7 of this book there is an interesting passage about the idea of divine descent among the Maoris, who seem to have benefited by it.

see, to apotheosis at Rome. In the oldest Rome the only trace of it known to me consists in the numerous taboos of the Flamen Dialis, which certainly look as if the priest of Jupiter had once been extremely precious if not divine, on account (such is the only explanation) of certain valuable magical powers attributed to him.[1] Dr. Frazer has done his best to prove that the divine king was native to Italy, in his *Lectures on the Early History of the Kingship*, and since then in the thirteenth chapter of the third edition of the *Golden Bough*.[2] But his arguments, as he himself allows, are purely conjectural, and rest almost entirely on legends contributed as "history" to instruct and amuse both peoples, by Greeks who in the third and second centuries B.C. began to take a lively interest in the affairs of Italy. The fact is that at present we know hardly anything of the religious ideas of the stocks from whom the Latins were descended, the people of the *terremare* who settled on the Alban hills and afterwards on the hills by the Tiber. The Etruscan contribution to Roman ritual and religion was a later adjunct, to which is due, as I said just now, the personation of Jupiter by the triumphing general, and perhaps the personation of dead ancestors by living men at funerals.[3] Before

[1] *R. R. Exp.* p. 108.
[2] *G.B.* ed. 3, vol. ii. of *The Magic Art*, ch. xiii. Cp. Cumont, *Astrology and Religion*, 180, where Manilius is quoted (i. 41).
[3] Polybius, vi. 53 foll.; *G.B.* ed. 3, vol. ii. p. 178, where the practice of the Roman nobiles at funerals is described as "masquerading as spirits." But the origin of the *imagines* is much too difficult a question to be thus lightly disposed of.

the age of the Etruscan dynasty at Rome it is certain that there was no iconic representation of the gods; such practices, therefore, as their representation by human beings was obviously impossible.

On the whole, then, we may conclude that there was little or nothing in the old Roman religious consciousness to bring Man into close relation to deity, and the same may probably be said of the old Italian religion generally. We may even guess that the idea of a man-god was repugnant to the *Sittlichkeit*[1] of the Roman, apart from his Etruscan inheritance; and this would be quite enough to explain why Augustus, who knew his people well, was so extremely cautious in handling the policy of imperial *apotheosis*. That policy, though controlled by Roman and Italian feeling, was really rooted in ideas and practices which were foreign and not native; and before concluding this lecture I must briefly refer to these. They have been the subject of much inquiry of recent years, in which our knowledge of Hellenistic history and literature has been steadily increased. In my next lecture I will go on to examine the facts of Roman apotheosis as exemplified under Caesar and Augustus.

The Greek custom of honouring renowned men as heroes after their death, and the later habit of so

---

[1] When I first wrote this passage Lord Haldane had not published his address to the American Bar, with its reference to the German word *Sittlichkeit*, and I searched in vain for an English word to express my meaning. The Roman repugnance to the worship of a man was not only a religious feeling but a part of the *Sittlichkeit* of the people.

honouring them even during their lifetime, as in the familiar instances of Brasidas, Lysander, Agesilaus, Alexander, Demetrius, Flamininus, and many more, might naturally suggest the theory that many or most gods had at one time been men. "In times which saw these human deities arise and pass away like fungi, the thought might easily occur that even the old gods of Greece might have been simply men deified by men."[1] This theory seems, however, to have originated in Egypt rather than in Hellas, and among the priests of the Egyptian religion. St. Augustine incidentally tells us that a certain high priest of this religion, Leo by name, told Alexander, as the king related in a letter to his mother, that not only heroes had been once men, but even the great deities, Zeus, Hera, and the rest.[2] Rather later, one Hekataeus in the time of Ptolemy I. gave expression to the same theory in a book about Egypt, where he lived; a work which is believed to be embodied in part in the first book of Diodorus Siculus.[3] He fancied that the sun, moon, and elements were the original and true gods, who might occasionally appear on earth in the form of sacred animals; but that apart from these were other earthly gods, who had originally been men, *e.g.* old Egyptian kings, who had been raised to godhead on account of their good

---

[1] I am here borrowing the forcible language of Döllinger in *The Gentile and the Jew*, vol. i. p. 364.
[2] Aug. *Civ. Dei*, viii. 5 and 27.
[3] For Hekataeus see Wendland, *Hellenistisch-römische Kultur*, ed. 2, p. 116 foll.

service to man. Such an one was Zeus; so too other polytheistic gods, with Isis and Osiris as their children. Wendland thinks that this theory was suggested by the political tendencies of the day, under the benevolent rule of the first Ptolemy; and this may very well have been so if we consider the inscriptions in honour of the king (Ptolemy, god and saviour) printed by him in an appendix to his valuable work.[1]

But Hekataeus did not attract popular attention in the same degree as his younger contemporary Euhemerus, whose name has always been associated with the theory. This man was also probably at home in Egypt, which may be looked on as the well-head of all these notions.[2] All that he did was to make yet another attempt to reckon with the popular belief in the gods, which had been shaken not only by Leo and Hekataeus, but by Epicurus, who denied their activity, and by the Stoics, who denied their personality. Euhemerus simply denied their existence as a species (so to speak) distinct from Man, and that is the point for us. I need not here go into his history or dilate upon his theory, of which the centre-point was the Cretan legend that Zeus was

[1] *Op. cit.* p. 406.

[2] In Egypt, as Wendland points out (p. 124), we find not only the later worship of kings, but the old Egyptian belief in god-kings, who were regarded as incarnations of Ra, Ammon, etc. It was natural that Alexander should be regarded as heir of the Pharaohs in this respect; and if he himself favoured the idea, it was easy enough even for Greeks to give effect to his wishes. His successors followed suit, all but the Macedonian kings, who did not need this support. But Wilcken seems to have proved (so my friend Mr. H. I. Bell assures me) that the cult of the Ptolemies was really Greek, not Egyptian, in its antecedents.

born and also died there. He treated divine history like human, giving accounts of reigns; Zeus, for example, had played much the same part as that which so astonished the world in Alexander.[1] Are we to take Euhemerus seriously, or was he merely amusing himself and others with imaginative romance? The answer seems to be on the whole that we must not exaggerate his serious influence. In Greece the process of degrading the gods had gone pretty far already, even for the common folk, and a historical romance of this kind would not do much more harm—if harm it is to be called. But we are more especially concerned with Rome, where the old faith in forceful *numina* was just then being revolutionised by Graeco-Etruscan anthropomorphic conceptions, which were decomposing the older more valuable ideas of deity. There the translation of Euhemerus by Ennius, executed perhaps only with a literary object in view, was much more serious in its result. Cicero uses strong language of it—he insists that it "penitus sustulisse deos."[2] He means that it cleared the ground for Epicureanism, with its gods indifferent to human life; he might also have said that by bringing humanity and divinity into the closest relation to each other, it also confirmed the growing desire to see divinity in great men. At Rome indeed that desire was not at work in the time

---

[1] Diodorus v. 41 foll.; Döllinger, *op. cit.* p. 365 note. Lactantius (i. 11) tells (from Ennius) of the "res gestae" of Zeus.
[2] *N.D.* i. 119.

of Ennius, nor for long after. But the Euhemerus of Ennius helped to make ready for a time when such a desire might arise, by squeezing the life out of the gods of the State, and substituting nothing for them.

Let us notice that the various currents of religious thought which I have been tracing to their sources, though some of them did not flow from genuine Italian fountain-heads, all contribute to one common reservoir, which is continually increasing in content— I mean *Individualism*. On reflection it will be seen that the belief in beings intermediate between man and god, the idea of divine descent, the primitive belief in the divinity of kings, and the new theory that gods were originally men, all have a tendency to exalt the importance of the individual, and his hold upon the reverence of his fellow-men. So too probably had another theory of this period, the Stoic idea that Man, if he realises his true nature fully, identifies himself with the nature of God.[1] Though there are weak points in this view as applied to man in general—for it seems to make God responsible for human wickedness,[2] yet as in practice it was taken as applying to great and good men only, it must have contributed to the exaltation of the individual in human life. Social life, too, in all this Hellenistic period favoured the same tendency; the constant wars, conquests, and revolutions threw the powerful man into ever greater prominence, and the poverty

---

[1] See *Religious Experience*, p. 368.
[2] Glover, *Conflict of Religions in the Early Roman Empire*, p. 97.

THE IDEA OF THE MAN-GOD

and distress of the Graeco-Roman world disposed the humbler folk to adore any leader of men who could and did procure them decent comfort and adequate bodily maintenance. The same tendency is to be found by the historical student in the fifteenth and sixteenth centuries, when the mediaeval forms of religion, like those of the ancient City-state, had gradually to give way before independence of individual thought, while the unceasing wars and other troubles, as in the older classical ages, were constantly throwing individual leaders into prominence. In each case the number of the *dramatis personae* of history greatly increases as these influences begin to tell. But in the ancient world we have one cause in action which I cannot trace in the middle ages; I mean the constant movement of the population, especially as the result of slavery in the last two centuries B.C. The individual element in the slave-population, though still apt to be crushed by ill-usage, was now freed from the fetters of the old group-associations, and the freedmen of Rome and other great towns were no longer bound by ancient traditions and prejudices.[1] They would readily take to new forms of religion; they would find congenial duty in the worship of a benevolent ruler, whether during or after his lifetime, as can be abundantly proved from the history of the Empire. They would also be attracted by the mystery religions, with their doctrines of the salvation of the individual soul, and

[1] See *Social Life in the Age of Cicero*, p. 231.

the endowment of the initiated person with godlike powers. This last belief is one not without importance for our subject, as illustrating the growing consciousness of a close relation between the human and the divine, and seems to be reflected in the Orphic language of the fourth *Eclogue* of Virgil, " Ille deum vitam accipiet." But it would lead me too far afield to go further into it here.[1]

Thus we arrive at last at the actual deification of man in the period I am dealing with. In Rome and Italy, as we have seen, this was not a natural growth of religion, as Boissier and others fancied long ago ; for there the deities were not thought of personally, and human individualism took long in developing. But elsewhere it was really natural, and the force with which it worked came gradually to react on Rome and Italy. In the great and good man, helping his subjects or his fellows, divinity revealed itself— so they thought in those days : " die Gottheit ist lebendig in ihnen erschienen."[2] Even the living king may be a " saviour," if he have wrought good works for the mass of mankind. To anticipate for a moment, Virgil never seems to speak of Augustus as divine unless he is thinking of him " as doing good service for men, as giving peace to the world after a century of anarchy."[3] And it may be, as Professor

[1] See *Virgil's Messianic Eclogue*, p. 63 foll., and S. Reinach's essay, reprinted in his *Cultes, mythes, et religions*, vol. ii. p. 66 foll. I may also refer to Reitzenstein's *Hellenistische Mysterienreligionen*, p. 34 foll.

[2] Wendland, *op. cit.* p. 127.

[3] I quote from a paper kindly sent me by Professor Conway on the teaching of Virgil, read to the conference of classical teachers in 1912, p. 15.

Conway suggests, that this conception of a *deus* did much to raise and purify the whole connotation of the word *deus*. But of course degeneracy was to follow, the result of the foolish pomp of a court, or the cruelty of a ruler, or the servility that some parts of a vast population could show towards their human masters. Even by the time of Cicero and Caesar the genuine feeling, rooted in gratitude and not in servility, had become more or less degraded in the Hellenistic world. Could it then be genuine at Rome? This question I will try to answer in the next lecture.

Let me briefly sum up what I have been saying. The Roman gods of the State could only be supposed to exist in and through the worship ordained by the State; on that point Varro and Cicero are clear. They would perish if the cult were neglected; and this was actually happening in the age of those writers. What then was to be done? The State could not exist without religion; such a thing was unthinkable for every ordinary citizen. To these men, too, the World-soul as a deity could not appeal, and attempts to force it into relation with the State by way of syncretism were not destined to succeed. Jupiter with his monotheistic tendency might have a chance; but he was already more or less damaged, and was soon to have a dangerous blow dealt him, as we shall see.

But there was another way, though not an easy one, to the discovery of a worship in the closest relation to the State, and a worship not likely to be soon neglected. The great and good man, the Scipio of his day—or the great and powerful man without the goodness—might be recognised as bearing the stamp of divinity, as having a divine spark within him; to him the old forms of cult might reasonably be transferred. This indeed had never been done before in Italy, and there was no room in the old Italian beliefs for the idea of a Man-god. But in the Eastern Mediterranean the idea and practice were both familiar, and they now began to invade Italy. Slowly and gradually, with the aid of Graeco-Etruscan ideas of the gods, and also of the truly Roman doctrine of Genius, they made way in the Italian cities, in spite of their incompatibility with the old Italian ideas of deity.

LECTURE V

DEIFICATION OF CAESAR

SUETONIUS, in a well-known sentence at the end of his life of Julius, distinguishes between what we may call the official divine honours voted to their dead master by the Senate, and the popular belief in his divinity. "In deorum numerum relatus est non ore modo decernentium sed et persuasione vulgi."[1] He refers mainly to what happened after Caesar's death, though not until nearly two years had passed; but the distinction holds good from the first appearance of the desire to deify a man at Rome, and will be useful to us throughout. The official process represents on the whole the restraining influence of the Roman State religion on the licence of unauthorised attempts at worship; this at least is fairly true from the death of Julius onwards. The official and the popular deification had indeed at first very little to do with each other. So far as I can see, the official decrees did not at first respond to any demand on the part of the populace, but were rather the independent

[1] Suet. *Iul.* 88.

action of one or more individuals in the Senate who were familiar with the deification of rulers in the Eastern Mediterranean. There is no evidence that the populace was stirred till after the assassination, and the appearance of the comet later in the same year.

This feeling of the people is, for the purposes of these lectures, more interesting than the official decrees; in the latter there may always be imitation, or concealed purposes, the cunning of individuals, or the desire of the great man for elevation to the position of a superman. The belief of the people, even of so motley a population as that of Rome, has something to tell us of the floating ideas of deity, as well as of the conditions of human life in that strange time. For to understand the Roman Caesar-worship as one would understand a plant, not merely examining those parts of it exposed to the light, but those which are beneath the soil from which the plant springs and by which it lives, it is necessary to be intimately familiar with the social history of Rome of the last two or three generations. We must study the upper classes; their system of education; their experience in wars and provincial government; their attitude towards the governed both in the city and in the provinces, and to the slave population and the trade in slaves; their loss of all genuine religious influences, together with their official maintenance of the old fabric of the State religion; and the growing sense among them that life and property were unsafe under the existing *régime*. Secondly, we must study the condition of the plebs of the city, and, so far as is possible, of other Italian towns. " In that slack and sordid age it is at least extremely doubtful whether either the person or the property of the lower class of citizen could be said to have been properly protected in the city. And the same anarchy prevailed all over Italy—from the suburbs of Rome, infested by robbers, to the sheep-farm of the great capitalist, where the traveller might be kidnapped by runaway slaves, to vanish from the sight of men without leaving a trace of his fate."[1] We have to bear in mind the nature and condition of that *colluvies omnium nationum*, the Roman populace, free or unfree, without a religion in which it could believe, and with the Government either suppressing the new emotional cults which might have satisfied it, or restricting them with a strong hand. We have to remember the uncertainty of the food supply and the coinage, and the way in which prominent individuals might make use of them for their own purposes.[2]

It is of course impossible here to go in detail into these questions. But those who study them will probably come to the conclusion that wherever we

[1] Quoted from *Social Life at Rome in the Age of Cicero*, p. 59.

[2] I believe that the chief cause of the anxiety about the corn-supply had originally been the fluctuation of prices, and that the legislation of C. Gracchus had as its main object the steadying of market values: see *English Hist. Rev.*, 1905, p. 221 foll., and compare Prothero, *English Farming*, p. 254 foll., for a similar policy of our own Government in the seventeenth and eighteenth centuries. But at the end of the Republican period the uncertainty of price and of supply was renewed by civil war.

look we find that everything in this age was making for monarchy, and that all that made for monarchy made also for a kind of quasi-religion closely associated with it—in other words, for the ascription of divinity to rulers. A *Sôter* was needed to put an end to all this distress and anarchy; and such saviours of men had too long been worshipped in the Mediterranean lands for such an one to escape apotheosis at Rome. Whether Julius did really appear in this light during his lifetime may be doubted. He was little known at Rome. He was too impartial, too cool-headed, as, for example, in the matter of the corn-doles.[1] Order indeed was restored by him; resistance was useless; if they could not entirely understand what he was about, they could at least feel the satisfaction of having a master. But before I examine closely the attempts to make a god of him, let me ask whether there are any precedents for the process known to us among the Romans.

We know that provincial governors had often had some kind of divine honours offered them in Greece and the East, a practice genuine enough no doubt at first, as in the case of Flamininus, but tending to become stereotyped, as we find it in Cicero's letters. But among the Romans themselves there had been sporadic instances, and more perhaps than we happen to know of. Scipio Africanus, as Mr.

---

[1] A statesman who could reduce the number of recipients of these doles from 320,000 to 150,000 (Suet. *Iul.* 41) would hardly have been spontaneously adored by the people.

Bevan remarks in his account of Roman deification,[1] had been looked on with something approaching to religious awe, and (as I may add here) after his death his statue was placed in the cella of the Capitoline temple, where he had been used to sit and contemplate the image of Jupiter. The next case is that of Metellus Pius, the colleague of Sulla in the consulship, and sent to Spain by him to put down a rising in Lusitania. In a passage of Sallust [2] we are told that when he arrived in Spain he was received by his friends with divine honours—" ture quasi deo supplicabatur." As there is no obviously sufficient reason for this, I am inclined to think that the incense was not an important feature of the show they arranged to welcome him with. More interesting is the quasi-adoration offered to Marius Gratidianus, praet. 86 B.C., of which we learn from Cicero, *de Officiis*, iii. 80. This man had done much to relieve the plebs from distress by an improvement in the coinage; " nemo unquam multitudini erat carior," he was a popular favourite. The story is a curious one, and illustrates in a remarkable way what I said just now about the tendency to monarchy and its inevitable accompaniment of divine honours. The edict about the coinage was the work of the whole collegium praetorum, of which Marius was only one member, and it was arranged that all of them should appear on the rostra to expound it; but Marius went straight up

---

[1] In Hastings's *Encyclopaedia of Religion and Ethics*, vol. iv. p. 529 B.
[2] Quoted by Macrobius iii. 13. 7.

and anticipated the rest. The result was that he was adored with incense and candles, and with many statues in the streets—"omnibus vicis statuae," says Cicero with his usual exaggeration. Lights and incense were features in the ordinary worship, but not features of great importance; and significant as the story is, we must not make too much of it. What it does seem to show is that when the populace believed in a Euergetes or Sôter they were apt to show their gratitude in terms of religion, if I may so express it, without perhaps meaning that the object of their veneration was in any sense really divine.

Passing to the cult of Caesar, I will first examine the evidence of fact; but I may just remark to begin with that there is little sign of any real interest taken in the matter by contemporaries.[1] Cicero mentions it only two or three times, twice jokingly in letters to Atticus, and once in his attack on Antony in the second *Philippic*. None of his or Caesar's friends allude to it in the surviving correspondence, nor does it appear in any other author of the time, Sallust, Cornelius Nepos, or the Caesarean military writers. Nor does the next age show any interest in it. If the fifth *Eclogue* has anything to do with it, which is doubtful, it must be taken as poetry only. Livy makes no allusion to it in his extant books, nor is there any in the epitome of his 116th book, nor in any writers who may have

---

[1] In a solitary inscription from Nola Caesar is called *deus* by a grateful *decurio* (*C.I.L.* x. 1271).

followed Livy, from Velleius and Valerius Maximus to Eutropius and Orosius. What we know is mainly derived from Dio Cassius, where we find it among the long lists of honours conferred on Caesar by the Senate, which may have been derived from the *acta senatus*. Whether Caesar himself was interested in it is at least doubtful. If he was ever caught by the idea of deification, it must have been when he was in Egypt and the East, and this is indeed possible. But if so, he must have looked on it merely as a piece of state-craft, necessary only where all rulers had been for so long looked on as above the common level of human nature. During his ten years in Gaul he could have known nothing of it; and if we can judge by his writings and the general course of his actions, he was too matter-of-fact to have any natural leaning towards what in Italy would be still unnatural and unmeaning. To the last all his friends seem to have looked on him as a very real human being.

I will take the progress of deification, for which the authorities have recently been conveniently put together by a writer in *Klio*,[1] in three periods : (1) up to the campaign of Munda, 45 ; (2) after the victory of Munda, and before Caesar's return to Rome ; (3) after his final return to Rome in the autumn of 45.

1. At the battle of Pharsalia Caesar gave as his battle-cry Venus *Victrix*, and vowed a temple to this deity, the reputed ancestress of the *gens* Julia.[2] This

[1] By Hubert Heinen in *Klio*, vol. xi. (1911), 129 foll.
[2] Appian ii. 63 ; Dio Cass. xliii. 22. 2.

was not indeed the only Roman family supposed to descend from the Trojan Aphrodite; the Memmii as well as Julii had already placed her head on their coins.[1] But when the temple came to be built in Caesar's forum it was dedicated to Venus *Genetrix*, of whom we thus hear for the first time. Henceforward the old Greek combination of Aphrodite and Ares begins to appear in the Roman form of Mars as pater Romuli, and Venus from whom the second Romulus was descended; there seems, as we shall see directly, to be some ground for believing that Caesar had no objection to appearing in this capacity of second founder. But the combination does not become obvious in his time; we have to go for it to Ovid's *Tristia*,[2] where the temples of Venus Genetrix and Mars Ultor are mentioned as standing close to each other in the Forum Augusti. This change of Venus Victrix to Venus Genetrix is almost the only sign we have of any interest taken by Caesar in the divinity of himself or his family; and it does not amount to much.

In 47 he was deified as Sôter and Euergetes in true Hellenistic fashion at Ephesus, from which port he embarked that year on his way back to Italy.[3] Then followed the African campaign; and before his return after Thapsus the Senate had begun to heap honours

---

[1] Wissowa, *Gesammelte Abhandlungen*, p. 15 foll.
[2] *Tristia*, ii. 295.
[3] *C.I.G.* 2957. For Sôter in the history of Greek and Hellenistic religion, see Hofer's article in Roscher. That Caesar sailed from Ephesus is in itself likely, and seems proved from an allusion in Cic. *Att.* xi. 24.

on him,[1] but had not suggested worship except by placing his chariot opposite to that of Jupiter on the Capitol, with a statue standing, or intended to stand, on a model of the world, and with an inscription calling him demi-god. This has been explained as an imitation of a statue of Attalus III. at Pergamum (whose statue, however, was erected on spoils and not on a conquered world)—a conclusion perhaps too hastily arrived at. In any case Caesar had the offensive inscription erased, as Dio himself tells us.[2] So far, then, we have found nothing to suggest any serious attempt at deification.

2. After the news of Munda arrived at Rome, when Caesar seemed fairly invincible, and the cause of his enemies hopeless, we learn from Dio of a new list of honours, and among them two religious ones of some significance. The Senate decreed that an ivory statue of Caesar should be carried in procession, with a chariot to itself, in the *ludi circenses*, along with those of the gods.[3] This is not an imitation of anything oriental, but an extension of a Roman custom in vogue since the introduction of iconic figures of the gods. Caesar had not yet returned; the Senate was responsible for this, and the Senate of this time is a mystery. At the same time it was

---

[1] Dio xliii. 14.
[2] Dio xliii. 14. 6. For the comparison with Pergamum see Domaszewski, *Abhandlungen*, 193.
[3] Dio xliii. 45. This may have had special reference to Caesar's expected triumph; but the *pompa* in which the images were carried was by this time extended to all *ludi circenses*; see Friedländer in Marquardt, *op. cit.* p. 508.

decreed that another statue should be placed in the temple of Quirinus on the Quirinal Hill. Here Quirinus must be understood as identical with Romulus—a point I referred to in the last lecture; the identification was recent, and became stereotyped under Augustus.[1] When Scipio's statue was placed in the cella Iovis the object was apparently to mark a close connexion between the man and the god, to whom Scipio had always been devoted; so here we may guess that the object was to suggest that a second founder of Rome had arisen, who must be placed in close relation with the original founder. In this there would be no necessary suggestion of deity; in fact it was contrary to all Roman usage to have two deities in a single temple, as we know from the story of Honos and Virtus in the Hannibalic War.[2] True, Dio tells us that the statue was inscribed Deo Invicto; if this was the fact, it was a scandalous innovation suggesting a pseudo-Mithraic origin; but Dio may be wrong, or the inscription may have been added later. Cicero twice alludes to this statue without recognising any attempt at deification; he was at Astura at the time, in grief for the loss of Tullia, but he had been told of it. Atticus's house was close to this temple, also to the neighbouring one of Salus; and in May Cicero wrote to him: "De Caesare vicino scripsi ad te, quia cognoram ex tuis

---

[1] See Hülsen-Jordan, *Röm. Topographie*, iii. 408.

[2] *The Religious Experience of the Roman People*, p. 328. Statues found in sanctuaries of Apollo, says Wilamowitz (*Apollo*, 26) represent men dedicated to the god, not the god himself.

litteris. Eum *sunnaon* Quirini malo quam Salutis." [1] He uses a Greek word because there was none in the Roman *ius divinum* for a temple-companion; but in June (*Att.* xiii. 28) he uses the word *contubernalis* for the same thing, again omitting all reference to divinity.[2] Read this letter as a whole, and this last fact becomes perfectly clear. Caesar is to him still a friend, and he laughs at the awkward attempts to bring him within range of divinity, of which Caesar himself could have as yet known nothing. There had, in fact, been very little so far to attract general attention to such attempts.

3. I now come to the third and last attempt at deification during Caesar's lifetime. This was after the beginning of the year 44, and was entirely due, so far as I can discern, to the influence in the Senate of the new consul Antony. Cicero later in the year ascribed to him a decree that a fifth day of the *ludi Romani*, i.e. in all probability September 19, should be added in honour of Caesar; [3] this was a *rogatio*, preceded, no doubt, by a *senatus consultum*. The inference is easy that all other such *rogationes*

[1] Cic. *Att.* xii. 45.

[2] "Quid, tu hunc de pompa, Quirini contubernalem, his nostris moderatis epistolis laetaturum putas?"

[3] Cic. *Phil.* ii. 110. The 13th (Ides) was the day of the *epulum Iovis* and the *dies natalis* of the great temple. The *ludi* probably began on the 15th originally (see *Roman Festivals*, p. 216, note 5): the day added in honour of Caesar may have been the fifth after this, viz. by Roman reckoning the 19th. Mommsen (*C.I.L.* i. ed. 2, 329), reckoning in the opposite direction, put Caesar's day on September 4, which I do not understand. September 19 was the date of the meeting of the Senate, on which day Antony attacked Cicero, and therefore the supposed date of the second *Philippic*. This fits in with the language of *Phil.* ii. 110.

were also proposed in the Senate by Antony. He, too, was to be a priest, a *flamen*, of a new Caesar-cult, a member of the new gild of Luperci Iuliani. It seems, then, that a serious attempt at deification was now being made, and by the very man from whom we might expect it, knowing as we do his later orientalism. We must also remember that Antony, after a period of disgrace, had just been restored to favour by Caesar, and might be trying to show his devotion. On the other hand, it is quite as likely, I think, that he was deliberately entering on a policy intended to ruin Caesar. He knew perfectly well that genuine Romans, even of the city, were not yet ripe for appreciation of a god-man; and that Caesar was not well enough known in Rome to be as yet accepted as Euergetes in his lifetime. I may be wrong, but I still think, as I long have thought, of Antony as Caesar's evil genius, playing him false and tempting him on; and I suspect an intrigue against Caesar between Antony and Cleopatra, who was in Rome at this time. Caesar was extremely busy himself, as we may see from the famous letter of Cicero describing his entertainment of the dictator; his mind was full of politics, of literature, and of military preparation, and I do not for a moment believe that he troubled himself much about his own worship.

On the other hand, von Domaszewski, in a short paper reprinted in his collected essays,[1] insists that

[1] *Abhandlungen*, p. 193. The author makes no attempt to survey the whole situation but examines a detail only, as he often does. In interpreting

Caesar was himself aiming at an oriental divine kingship, on the analogy of that of the kings of Pergamum. There is a certain amount of likeness between the cult at Pergamum and the honours reported by Dio Cassius; but Dio is far from being above suspicion, and all the circumstantial evidence is against this theory. There is no special reason for the choice of Pergamum for imitation; there is no contemporary allusion to any such attempt to orientalise Roman worship, and it is wholly incompatible with all we know about the character and temperament of Caesar. It is possible that Antony, who had had much experience already of the East and Egypt, had in his mind the Hellenistic divine king when he made the proposals to which Cicero alluded eighteen months later in the second *Philippic*; but there was nothing among them that was specially Oriental. Domaszewski is, I think, obsessed by his revival of the generally discredited statement of Dio that Caesar was made Jupiter Julius,[1] which, if it means anything, means that he now became an incarnation of Jupiter, retaining his own gentile name as a cult-title. It is absolutely incredible that such

---

Cic. (*Phil.* ii. 110) he makes the mistake of putting the *epulum Iovis* on the 15th instead of the 13th of September, *i.e.* the Ides.

[1] Dio xliv. 6. 2. Cicero's language in *Phil.* ii. 110 seems to make it clear that Antony's *flaminium*, which is often described as specially analogous to the *flaminium Diale*, had nothing to do with Jupiter, much less with any Jupiter Julius. "Est ergo flamen, ut Iovi, ut Marti, ut Quirino, sic Divo Julio Marcus Antonius?" It cannot be proved from these words either that Caesar was Jupiter Julius, or that Antony was a new Flamen Dialis. Antony was, or had been, simply the *flamen* of Divus Julius. In 40 he became Flamen Julianus afresh, if Plutarch is to be believed (*Ant.* 33).

a violation of all Roman religious practice and language should have remained unnoticed in all contemporary literature, when Cicero at least would have had abundant opportunity of making scathing remarks about it. If it were worth while to look for an explanation, we might find it in the triumph after Munda, and the practice of decking out the triumphator in the guise of Jupiter. But Domaszewski need not be taken seriously, so far at least as Caesar himself was concerned. "The *dominus* and *deus* of the Orient found his way into the *urbs aeterna*" sounds well, but is not history.

So far we have found nothing to indicate that the *populace* was affected by the idea of a man-god; as I have hinted, they did not know Caesar well, and had received no great benefits from him. But the murder and the reading of the will undoubtedly excited them. If we follow Dio,[1] we must accept the story that a popular attempt to proclaim the dead Caesar a god was made the very evening of the murder, and had to be put down by the consuls, Antony and Dolabella, who were responsible for the peace of the city and also for the maintenance of Roman religious law. The statement, however, is not necessarily true, and the only interest to be found in it is the implied assumption that even a Roman mob, if excited, might find a religious outlet for that excitement, and the moral that even an Antony must keep an official hold on all attempts to introduce the cult of a new god.

[1] Dio xliv. 51.

The comet which appeared during the games given by Octavian in the summer, and the eclipse of the sun in the autumn, served the purpose of keeping up the excitement, and the belief that Caesar was something more than mortal. Pliny has preserved the account of the comet given by Augustus himself, containing the following words of importance for us : " Eo sidere significari volgus credidit Caesaris animam inter deorum immortalium numina receptam, quo nomine id insigne " (*i.e.* the star) simulacro capitis eius, quod mox in foro consecravimus, adiectum est."[1] Here we may note parenthetically that the religion of astrology, which M. Cumont has so admirably sketched of late, is now seen making its entry into Rome. And at this same time began that sense of dejection and mental distress which Sallust and Livy reflect in their prefaces, and Horace in his 16th epode and elsewhere ; this too no doubt contributed to the general desire to be right with the Powers above, and among them now the victim of the assassins. It became necessary to control this abnormal feeling, according to the tradition of Roman government, of which our best illustration is their policy during the second Punic War, described in my fourteenth Gifford Lecture.[2] If the populace persuade themselves that Caesar has become a god, the belief must be blessed and restricted by an official sanction.

January 1, 42, nearly two years after the murder,

[1] Plin. *N.H.* ii. 94.   [2] *Religious Experience*, ch. xiv.

is the date of the first Roman official ordinance that made a dead man into a god.[1] A temple was promised to Divus Iulius, now numbered among the gods of the State. Any former attempts at oriental Kingworship, such as we have noticed just now, were done away and forgotten, and Divus Iulius was treated like any other deity in the Roman pantheon. Owing to various hindering causes the temple was not consecrated till after the return of Augustus in 29 B.C., when on August 18 the *aedes Divi Iulii in foro* was placed on the same footing as other temples, and provided with a Flamen and *feriae publicae* on its *dies natalis*.[2] The cult is thus regulated in proper Roman fashion, and taken out of reach of the orientalising innovators. The arch-orientaliser, Antony, was a party to this; but he had for some time, since the death of Caesar, been returning to Roman ways, suggested both by the obvious policy of the moment, and also no doubt by the influence of his colleagues, one of whom was *pontifex maximus*, and the other the inheritor of Caesar's rational temperament. Thus whatever was really bad or degrading in the worship of a living man was happily avoided : to think of a dead man as endowed with deity, as the natural result of his good works on earth, and as sanctioned and legally ordered by the State, was on the whole elevating rather than lowering in its moral effects. Much that I have already said in the last lecture will

[1] *C.I.L.* ix. 2628 ; Wissowa, *R.K.* ed. 2, p. 342.
[2] *Ib.* p. 343. Augustus mentions the consecration in his *Res Gestae* (*Mon. Anc.* iv. 2).

explain or excuse it; it is far from being out of harmony either with the Roman idea of Genius or with the Stoic doctrine of the scale of existence. The thinking Roman might possibly smile at it, doubting the immortality of the soul as the Dictator himself, like so many others, had doubted it; but as a Roman citizen even he could find no fault with the attribution of divinity—a kind of super-humanity—to the most wonderful of all Romans. There was nothing oriental or meretricious about the conception of Divus Iulius; this was not a mystery religion, and there was nothing mysterious about it. It meant the erection of a temple in the forum, with a *dies natalis* and a temple staff; it was an act of policy, but also of gratitude and commemoration. It is possible, as Professor Conway has suggested of the same policy under Augustus, that its contribution to the idea of deity was wholesome rather than the contrary.[1]

The ascription of divinity to Augustus is far more familiar ground than that of Julius, and I only propose to deal with it here so far as it bears on our subject—the ideas about deity in the Rome of this age.

In the first place, it clearly shows the strength of Roman and Italian feeling as distinct from that of the orientalisers. Augustus never appeared as deity in his lifetime, except here and there in private worship. He seized on the Roman idea of Genius, neglected by Antony in the last months of Julius's life, and by placing his own Genius between the

[1] *On the Teaching of Vergil*, p. 15 (kindly sent me by the author).

images of the *Lares compitales* he fairly turned the flank of all direct attempts to deify a living man. He wished no doubt to be thought of as *pater patriae, euergetes*, saviour, like the Ptolemies and others, but he will have nothing that can strictly be called worship publicly offered him. The best way to realise this is to reflect that he was a member of all the great priesthoods, and eventually became *pontifex maximus*, after duly waiting for the long-expected vacancy; that is, he was the chief member of the public officials of Roman cult, a position absolutely incompatible with godhead. At the greatest of all his religious ceremonials, the *ludi saeculares* of 17 B.C., we know for a fact that he officiated as a priest, together with his very human helpmate, M. Agrippa.[1] Such facts as these make it unwise to attach any weight to the story of Suetonius that he on one occasion at least masqueraded as Apollo at a party where his friends represented other gods.[2] Even if true, which is

---

[1] *C.I.L.* vi. 32323, line 107 and elsewhere.

[2] Suet. *Aug.* 70; see *Classical Review*, 1913, pp. 18 and 87. More serious is the statement that there were statues of Augustus in the guise of Apollo, if these were publicly exhibited. Pelham, *e.g.* (*Essays in Roman History*, p. 104), says that in the great hall of the *area Apollinis* on the Palatine there was a statue of Augustus fifty feet high with the attributes of Apollo; and Pelham was rarely wrong. But in this case he made a mistake. He quotes a passage (Plin. *N.H.* xxxiv. 43), in which it is stated that in the library of the temple of Augustus himself, a temple not dedicated till long after his death, there was a "Tuscanicus Apollo" fifty feet high. It would seem likely, in spite of the word *tuscanicus*, that this was the statue alluded to by Suetonius, *Vita Tiberii*, 74, " et amplitudinis et artis eximiae," brought from Syracuse at the end of Tiberius's reign, to be placed in the library of a new temple. We may be quite sure that Augustus would never have ventured to place his own statue in the consecrated ground of Apollo if it were clothed with the attributes of that deity.

doubtful, it would not affect his notion of his own divinity. And again the very fact that it fell to him to dedicate in 29 the temple of Divus Iulius that had been vowed thirteen years before, shows that he could not be himself then thinking of his own divinity as a living man. The strength of Roman feeling was far too strong for such notions to prevail even among the mongrel plebs of the city. It was only in the course of his long principate that signs begin to appear of the inevitable desire to turn honour into worship. These have been admirably put together by the late Professor Pelham in his essay on the domestic policy of Augustus,[1] and I need not pursue them in detail. In my opinion they prove no change in the attitude of Augustus to apotheosis, and must be treated as exceptions, not as the rule. Here again we may argue back from the policy of Tiberius, who was in so many points the faithful interpreter of the wishes of Augustus; he would encourage the cult of the dead *princeps*, but would on no account allow

---

No doubt, according to abundant precedent, he might combine his own likeness on coins with those attributes: Cohen, i. Aug. No. 117, quoted by Pelham, *loc. cit.* And Servius (*Ecl.* iv. 10) vaguely says that there was a statue of Augustus with all the insignia of Apollo, but does not tell us whether it was made in his lifetime. The devotion of Augustus to Apollo is of course a proved fact; but all the evidence for it needs to be warily handled.

[1] Pelham, *Essays on Roman History*, p. 108. He mentions (1) the gossip conveyed in Suetonius, 74 foll., which when examined contains nothing of real value; (2) a single case of *devotio* to the *numen Augusti*, recorded by Dio two centuries later; (3) the only substantial evidence—the traces of priesthoods and altars to Augustus dating from his lifetime. The epigraphical evidence is given in note 9, p. 108, and except at Pompeii is unimportant.

himself to be the object of worship. We may take it as certain that during his long reign Augustus enforced the principle that the worship of a living man was a thing impossible in Roman religious law; and that he wished to be honoured as a sovereign (to quote Professor Pelham), but not as a god. However closely he might allow himself to be brought into relation with the gods of the State, however frequently he might use the machinery of the State religion for lifting himself into an abnormal in the eyes of the plebs as their supporter and benefactor, he never gave way to that oriental idea of man-worship which had perhaps possessed the mind of the more voluptuous Antony.

It may perhaps be argued that the evidence of the literature of the age disproves this contention; we naturally think of certain passages both of Virgil and Horace, almost too familiar to need quotation in full.[1] But you have only to examine them to see that they represent Augustus not as a deity, but as having the germ of a deity in him, which may be developed at his death; and that the farthest length they go is to assume proleptically in imagination that this development has already taken place. Take for instance the lines at the end of the first *Georgic*—

> Iam pridem nobis caeli te regia, Caesar,
> Invidet,[2]

---

[1] Wendland, *op. cit.* p. 143, note 7.
[2] *Georg.* i. 503.

and Horace's

> Serus in caelum redeas, diuque
> Laetus intersis populo Quirini.[1]

Some lines in the second book of Ovid's *Tristia* are perhaps more interesting and less familiar, written when the other two poets had long been dead; for we know that Ovid would then have naturally been careful not to write anything that might annoy Augustus or tend to interfere with his public policy.[2]

> Per mare, per terras, per tertia numina iuro,
> Per te *praesentem* conspicuumque *deum*:
> Hunc animum favisse tibi, *vir maxime*, meque,
> Qua sola potui, mente fuisse tuum.
> Optavi, peteres caelestia sidera tarde,
> Parsque fui turbae parva precantis idem,
> Et pia tura dedi pro te, cumque omnibus unus
> Ipse quoque adiuvi publica vota meis.

Here is indeed a curious mélange of humanity and deity: I know no passage that shows so well the characteristics of that borderland. Ovid begins by audaciously including Augustus as *praesens deus* in his attestation of loyalty (we can hardly call this rhetorical artifice a true oath); and in the very next line he expressly calls him a man, *vir maxime*. " I prayed," he goes on, " that you might live long on earth—long delay the assumption of godhead: and with this end I offered incense for your safety." Augustus is throughout the poem plainly a man, but

---

[1] *Odes*, i. 2. 45. Cp. *C.I.L.* x. 3757 (*Carm. Epigr.* no. 18), "Nam quom te Caesar tempus exposcet deum caeloque repetes sedem."

[2] *Tristia*, ii. 53 foll.

has the spirit (or germ) of a divine being in him, waiting for realisation at the moment of his departing this life.[1]

But, as I said, once or twice the poets proleptically represent the realisation as having already taken place, striking a false note, as it inevitably seems to us. "Quos inter Augustus recumbens purpureo *bibit* ore nectar" does not fail to offend, if we thus read the present tense, with many MSS., in Horace, *Odes*, iii. 3. 12. And Virgil had already struck the same discord in the invocation prefixed to the first *Georgic:* It is indeed just possible that Augustus had in some way consented to be reckoned, by those who had the fancy for it, as belonging to the species demi-god, even in his lifetime; for these were now commonly believed to have attained their position by their good works. Cicero, as I have pointed out, had expressed this belief long ago in the *Somnium Scipionis*; and Tacitus was to express it again in the chapter to which I alluded in my last lecture, where he sneers at Tiberius for lacking the ambition to rise above the plane of man's ordinary honour.[2]

---

[1] Hor. *Odes*, iv. 5. 31 foll., suggests the same odd mixture of man and deity—the deity as yet imperfectly realised.

[2] The *locus classicus* in Latin literature is Cic. *N.D.* ii. 62. "Suscepit autem vita hominum consuetudoque communis, ut beneficiis excellentes viros in caelum fama ac voluntate tollerent. Hinc Hercules, hinc Castor et Pollux, hinc Aesculapius, hinc Liber etiam . . . hinc etiam Romulus, quem quidem eundem esse Quirinum putant. Quorum cum remanerent animi atque aeternitate fruerentur, dii rite sunt habiti, cum et optimi essent et aeterni." Mayor (ii. p. 169) detects Posidonius here, which is likely enough. But after Ennius and Euhemerus there was perhaps a Roman tendency to believe in heroes after the Greek model.

On the whole, I would conclude from these and other passages in the poets that Augustus and all his sane advisers had a strong conviction of the unwisdom of ascribing real divinity to a living man in Rome or Italy. He felt this to be out of harmony with Roman and Italian ideas, out of harmony too with his own wishes and instincts; preferring, as he showed at his *ludi saeculares*, and in the hymn written for that festival at his order, to be *deorum cultor* rather than *deus* or *divus*. But as poets may be allowed some licence of expression not vouchsafed to ordinary men, we find a tendency among them to think of him as something more than man, as having divine seed in him, which puts him in the position of a hero even while he lives, as a doer of great works and as the saviour of his people; as destined also after death to dwell among the real deities in their celestial abode. Thus the conscience of the Italian is not wounded, while the non-Italian part of the city population—the foreign readers of Roman poets, if such there were—would recognise a tone in the music to which they were no strangers.

With the worship of Caesar in the provinces I am not here closely concerned, for it bears quite indirectly on our subject. But I will conclude this lecture with a few words about two points in it.

First, as to its conjunction with the cult of Rome as a deity, which is found in Greece and the East, less frequently in the West.[1] It is important to

[1] Toutain, *Les Cultes païens, etc.*, vol. i. ch. ii.

notice that the cult of Roma existed long before the Empire; Smyrna began it in 195 B.C., and was followed by Alabanda in Caria, and in 163 by Rhodes, where a colossal image of the Roman people was placed in the sanctuary of the protecting deity of the city, Athena.[1] If we ask what idea of divinity this implies, we may answer that the worship of the protecting fortune (Tyche) of a city was common enough in Greece, and that it was only going a step further to add that of the one overwhelming power in the Mediterranean. But there was probably another feature in it which is not so obvious, and which grows on our attention more and more as we find this cult associated with that of the Senate, then (or at the same time) with that of the reigning emperor, his *numen*, genius, etc. I mean that the actual conception of the divine or superhuman power in Roma becomes of less importance than the mental attitude of the worshipper; in other words, we do not so much need to inquire what sort of a deity this was thought to be, as to assure ourselves of the desire of the provincials to recognise the overwhelming strength, the irresistible force of organisation, which that name implied. These cities of Greece and Anatolia needed a means of expressing their feeling publicly, and it was natural to them to find it in the language and action of religion; but the nature of the deity concerned was the least important part of it. They applied to Rome, as later on to her provincial

[1] Polyb. xxxi. fragm. xvi. 4 (Hultsch).

governors, and then to her emperors, the language and action in which they had always been able to express publicly their faith, reliance, veneration—in a single Greek word, soon to be used in nobler contexts, their πίστις. They might realise, or, as we say now, visualise the object of their faith, by stamping an image on their coins, or placing a statue in their temples; but this was no essential matter of the cult, nor (if I am right) did they look on these as they had once looked on statues of Artemis or Athene; the essence of the cult was now less objective than subjective. The objective idea of deity waxes dim and vague all over the Mediterranean world, and what is now called by that name is really a desire to own and propitiate the earthly power on which your life and happiness depend.[1] It is characteristic of this tendency that Tiberius, who made so much of the Senate, succeeded in substituting it for Roma in many cities of Asia Minor.

What I have said about Dea Roma and its suggestion of divinity in the provinces applies in great measure to the Caesar-worship that accompanied it, *i.e.* to the cult of the *living* Caesar. I am not directly concerned with it as it appears in the eastern provinces, where its roots were fixed deep in the soil of Hellenistic thought and practice, and where there may have lingered some ancient traditional belief in the divinity of an all-powerful man. But I must say a very few

---

[1] Wissowa, *R.K.* ed. 2, 339. He notes the word "πίστις" in connexion with Dea Roma in the East: see note 2 on p. 339. It is used to mean a mutual confidence in good relations: so it seems to be in Diod. xxvii. 5. Cp. Plut. *Flam.* xvi. (hymn to Flam.).

words about it as we see it in the western or Latin-speaking provinces, where it derives directly from Italy.

Here the evidence is purely epigraphical; literature hardly makes a contribution. Just now we have good facilities for using the evidence of inscriptions, for M. Toutain, in his *Cultes païens dans l'Empire romain*, has analysed them with skill and good sense, and other writers, *e.g.* W. Otto in Pauly-Wissowa (article on "Genius"), have investigated particular points. In this way it has been made extremely probable that the growth of Caesar-worship in these provinces is so greatly *varied* in form that it can hardly have been the result of imperial organisation, but must rather have arisen independently in each locality—an important point for us. It was not a religion imposed from without, but a subjective expression of confidence (*fides* we may call it in the West) by the Romanised provincials and Italian residents. The worship of dead Caesars here is not of importance for us, nor was it common in the western provinces; but that of the Genius or Numen Augusti, whether combined or not with Dea Roma, or (as was frequently the case) in quaint juxtaposition with local deities, taken, as I think it should be, as signifying the Genius or Numen of the *living* Caesar, is shown by the inscriptions to have been a very real force in the West. The question for us is simply: "What kind of a deity does it suggest as the object of worship?" I believe that, as in the case of Dea Roma, the whole force of the worship lies in the worshipper and not in the deity. Genius or Numen Augusti is no more than a convenient peg to hang your faith on—your feeling of confidence in and reverence for the great system of government and civilisation of which you are a part. Incidentally it is a useful guarantee for the government that this faith is held and kept; but among the people who thus hold and keep it it is a spontaneous expression of belief, not in a deity, *but in something which you can treat as such.* It is based on the same principle as the application of Genius, Numen, Fortuna, Tutela, Virtus, and other such abstractions, to particular parts or institutions of the empire. These all seem to signify the *permanent force* of some inevitable institution deserving of the deepest respect and reverence, which can be expressed in terms of religion. The word adopted by Domaszewski, in his work on the religion of the Roman army, is a good one—*Lebensgeist*, the living spirit of empire in all its many manifestations. But this was not a deity in the proper sense of the word; it is the Latin language lending its old religious expressions to give articulation to an idea that was not strictly religious. Had these expressions possessed, in the imperial age, a real *Lebensgeist* of their own in a religious sense, they would surely have survived the empire in one form or another. But so far as I know, they vanished at the cock-crow of a new era, with all the paraphernalia of the religious or quasi-religious side of imperial organisation.

LECTURE VI

DEGRADATION OF THE IDEA OF DEITY IN THE AUGUSTAN AGE

So far we have not had to notice any marked degeneracy in the theology, if it can so be called, of the last century B.C. We did not find it in the religion of the family, nor in the monotheistic ideas beginning to gather round the name of the old heaven-god. The current beliefs about Fortuna had their bad side, but it was just on that side that Fortuna was least distinctly of divine nature. Again, in the rise of the conception of the Man-god—in the recognition of a divine element in Man which under certain conditions may claim worship from ordinary men, it may be that we should see rather elevation than degeneracy, though here too there were ugly features which are apt to make us look askance on the whole tendency. But in the dead or dying gods of Graeco-Roman polytheism, and especially in the use made of them in literature, there was a real source of danger for the germs of a nobler theology; and of this I must say something before I bring these lectures to a close.

In Greece this danger had been present for

centuries, ever since the first editing of the Homeric poems [1]; though checked by certain more wholesome influences so long as the City-state, with its guardian deities, had real life left in it. At Rome it was in the main the result of the importation of Greek anthropomorphic ideas of the gods, with the "serio-comic" mythology that naturally accompanied them; a transference, that is, from a soil from which the Olympians had once drawn some sap of real religion, to one quite strange to them, in which anthropomorphic plants used not to grow at all, and where consequently mythology was almost unknown. For mythology is the work of reflection; "it is when the community has time and inclination to reflect upon its gods and their doings that mythology arises." [2] But the old Romans had neither leisure nor inclination to reflect on the doings of their *numina*, which were not thought of as being in the likeness of man, and therefore did not suggest reflection. But when the Olympians came from Greece to Rome, they had been so long subjected to the mythological process that they were already stripped of any really religious attributes they may ever have claimed. No doubt there had been a religious force in them, which we can see, as Gilbert Murray says,[3] "if we rid our minds of trivial mythology." But for all but the best minds of Rome it was the lowest aspect of them that attracted

---

[1] See Gilbert Murray's *Rise of the Greek Epic*, ed. 2, pp. 277 foll., esp. p. 283.
[2] Jevons, *Idea of God in Early Religions*, p. 53.
[3] Gilbert Murray, *Four Stages of Greek Religion*, p. 94.

attention; they were no better than men, as gods must be if they are to be really gods, and in most cases they were worse. This makes advance on the lines of polytheism impossible; when once gods are degraded, they must drop out of religion.[1]

In Roman literature these gods are like peas shrunk and dead in a pod which still retains something of its old freshness. Even allegory, so freely used in this age and the following, especially by the Stoics,[2] and the main resource of those who wished to keep the Olympians alive, is not here, except in an occasional moral lesson like that of Phaethon. And worship had not then the advantage of being combined with a genuine feeling for the plastic arts.

I may digress for a moment to explain this last point a little more fully. Professor Gardner, in his *Grammar of Greek Art*, contends that in the best days of Olympianism the gods became not only more human, but more humane and righteous.[3] Then the Greek artist, following this lead, added a certain degree of moral and spiritual elevation to mere physical beauty. The types of god and goddess grew apart from those of the athlete and the mortal

---

[1] Jevons, *op. cit.* p. 36.

[2] Gilbert Murray, *Four Stages, etc.*, p. 146. Cp. Flinders Petrie, *Personal Religion in Egypt*, 119 foll. Allegory is frequent in Augustan sculpture, *e.g.* in that of the Ara Pacis.

[3] Gardner, *Grammar of Greek Art*, p. 103. Cp. E. Gardner, *Religion and Art in Ancient Greece*, p. 88. "To look upon such an image helped the worshipper as much as any service or ritual to bring himself into communion with the goddess, and to fit himself to carry out her will" (*i.e.* as an Athenian citizen).

woman. "They are touched by the light of another world." The best of these types did not violate the canon that gods, to be really gods, must be thought of as superior to man; they were ideal men, and something more. Thus they could stimulate men, in a way we can feel rather than explain, to high ideas of social life and duty; thus it was perhaps that Epicurus thought it possible for men to be the better for the contemplation of his gods, which were conceived in the likeness of ideal men.[1] When Quintilian said of the Zeus of Pheidias that it added something to the received religion,[2] he meant perhaps that the contemplation of it roused noble thoughts in the mind, thoughts of the union of all Greek hearts. But at Rome there was nothing in sculpture, even after the fashion had arisen of collecting Greek masterpieces, to compare with the moral splendour of the Zeus of Olympia; hardly anything to save the idea of God from the disintegrating acids of literature and mythology. The statue of Jupiter in his Capitoline cella is the only example we can think of, and the story of the great Scipio entering that cella every morning before daylight is the only trace, so far as I know, of the influence of plastic art on Roman character—and even that is not without suspicion.

So the one redeeming feature of the Olympian system was absent when that system came to Rome. When Augustus built a magnificent temple to Apollo on the Palatine, with the god as the sun, driving his

[1] *Religious Experience*, p. 359.   [2] Quoted by Gardner, *l.c.*

four-horse chariot, on its *fastigium*,[1] are we to suppose that he impressed the Roman world with any kind of religious feeling? I find no trace of such a feeling, and I altogether doubt it. There is of course abundant religious reference in Augustan art, *e.g.* in the sculptures of the Ara Pacis and the corslet of the great Prima Porta statue of Augustus. But I do not see how it could have been religiously impressive for the beholders, as well as interesting to the sculptor and his employer. But let us go a little more closely into the evidence for the Roman conception of Augustus's favourite deity; for beyond doubt he did wish to impress his own devotion on the Roman mind. The mere fact that such a man should have thought this possible is worth attending to, for he knew, if any one did, what the Roman religious mind was capable of. For once, I think, he was mistaken; misled by a quaint enthusiasm for the god who had looked down on his triumph at Actium.

Apollo is a good example of the killing power of the conventional use of divine names in literature. True, he had never been a great figure in the Roman world; he originally came in as a god of healing; his connexion with oracles and the Sibylline books was not matter of general interest, I think, in early Rome. As god of music and poetry he only began to be known when poetry and plays (translated from the Greek) became familiar; but by the time of

---

[1] Propertius iii. 28; cp. *Religious Experience*, p. 445.

Augustus this was practically the only light in which he was regarded by the ordinary Roman. The downright and intensely human Catullus does not trouble himself about Phoebus at all ; nor of course does Lucretius. If you try to think of any passage of Cicero in which he is mentioned, apart from one or two mythological chapters in the *de Nat. Deorum*, you may find some difficulty ; in the letters, the nearest approach to a recognition of him as a Roman god is a letter to Terentia from her husband about his health, in which he bids her sacrifice to Apollo and Aesculapius, because he feels a little better.[1] But in the Augustan poetry we find Apollo everywhere, not as a deity of medicine but of the poet's art, and in fact constantly as a mere synonym for poetry.[2] We may take an example among a thousand from the *Culex*, which we now believe to be Virgil's, and which I believe to have been written very early in his life,[3] so that it may be one of the first Latin examples we have of this literary convention : its invocation begins :

---

[1] *Fam.* xiv. 7.
[2] A good example in Ovid, *Ars Am.* ii. 493 foll. :—
    Haec ego cum canerem, subito manifestus Apollo
      Movit inauratae pollice fila lyrae :
    In manibus laurus, sacris induta capillis
      Laurus erat : vates ille videndus adit.
[3] Skutsch, *Aus Vergils Frühzeit*, p. 130. I agree with Skutsch (p. 131, note 2) that the epithets *sanctus* and *venerandus* applied to Octavius at the beginning of the *Culex* could not have been applicable in common use to *any* boy, and I feel confident that the boy in question must have been Caesar's nephew when really a boy, and when Virgil, who was seven years older, was not more than twenty.

> Latonae magnique Iovis decus, aurea proles,
> Phoebus erit nostri princeps et carminis auctor
> Et recanente lyra fautor. . . .

So too a while later in *Ecl.* iii. 62 :

> Et me Phoebus amat ; Phoebo sua semper apud me
> Munera sunt, lauri et suave rubens hyacinthus.

This is from the fifth Eclogue of Theocritus, and it is from the Alexandrian poetry in fact that most of the trouble comes. Phoebus is being used as a name and a symbol, without reality of godhead. " Sic me servavit Apollo," wrote Horace in his early days, uninfected as yet by the Augustan Apollinism, and still able to indulge his sense of humour. It is interesting to turn on to the later odes and the *Carmen saeculare*, to see what amount of vitality he can give to the newly established god of the Palatine. Every one must judge for himself ; personally I can find no life at all in the Apollo of these passages. In the *Carmen* he seems to me utterly lifeless ; but in the closely related sixth ode of Book iv., where Horace is addressing the members of the choir that he is training for the great Ludi, he puts a little human affection for this " spirit of poetry " as we should call it, into his verses :

> Spiritum Phoebus mihi, Phoebus artem
> Carminis nomenque dedit poetae.

As a modern poet might speak of the spirit of poetry, so did the Augustan poets speak of Apollo ; they do not really mean a god, at all, but clothe an abstraction in the conventional language of Greek anthropomorphism. I think that this treatment of the name destroyed any real chance Apollo might have had of useful life at Rome, just as the use of Jupiter and the rest as machinery in the *Aeneid* may have damaged them all for ever. Even Jupiter, I think, never recovered from this treatment, as a theological conception;[1] and any chance he had of becoming the centre of a real religious system such as that of the Stoics, was destroyed by the *Aeneid*, the *pietas* of whose hero is indeed nominally due to him, but in reality to the decrees of fate.

For Apollo there was indeed a chance, but he was already too decrepit when it came to him. He had long been associated with the sun, or even definitely identified with it, as at Delphi under the name Phoibos.[2] Sun-worship as a religion can undoubtedly be a reality; and now Apollo was once more to have the chance of amalgamation with the centre of such a religion. It is not unlikely that in the fourth *Eclogue*, where the god appears as a more religious being than elsewhere in Virgil, there is a tinge of this sun-worship at the back of the poet's mind.[3] M. Cumont might, I think, have suggested, in his lectures on *Astrology and Religion*,[4]

---

[1] On this point I enlarged in *Social Life at Rome in the Age of Cicero*, p. 341 foll.

[2] Gilbert Murray, *Four Stages*, etc., p. 70.

[3] On *Ecl.* iv. 10 ("tuus iam regnat Apollo"). Cf. Mayor in *The Messianic Eclogue*, p. 122.

[4] *Astrology and Religion*, p. 86.

that Augustus anticipated, or would have liked to anticipate, the sun-worship of the later empire. It is remarkable that as early as the battle of Bedriacum in A.D. 69, Vespasian's soldiers saluted the rising sun with loud shouts after the Syrian custom familiar to them in the East.[1] I think that Augustus must have supplied the necessary stimulus to this revived aspect of Apollo; both he and Tiberius were converts to astrology, which had come in chiefly as the work of the philosophical wizard Posidonius. But Phoebus Apollo himself could not survive; he gave way to the sun, in spite of Augustus. Plutarch, in writing of these things, is disposed to think that in his time Apollo was already giving way to the sun in Greece. "The Sun hath caused all people to forget Apollo, by diverting their attention, by means of the sense, from the real to the apparent."[2] In the western provinces, thanks to the labours of M. Toutain, we have the evidence of the *C.I.L.* collected and commented on.[3] But the evidence of the inscriptions is not clear or consistent. We find that Apollo survived, rarely as the Sun, more often as the Latin name for a native god of medicine, though his attribute is always the lyre. He is most frequently a physician's deity in the south and south-east of Gaul.[4] But on the whole it is pretty clear that the Augustan revival failed to secure him immortality; he

---

[1] Tac. *Hist.* iii. 24, quoted by Cumont, p. 161.
[2] *Pyth. Resp.* xii. Already, in the oracle about the *ludi saeculares*, Apollo is the sun; Zosimus v. 16: καὶ Φοῖβος Ἀπόλλων, ὅστε καὶ ἥλιος κικλήσεται ...
[3] *Cultes païens,* i. 314 foll.   [4] *Op. cit.* i. 318.

had no real root in the minds of any part of the population.

Mars is another good example of the killing of a deity, once full of life, mainly by literary convention. So entirely has Mars become, both in prose and poetry, a synonym for war, that even in the warlike *Aeneid* he is hardly recognisable as a deity. He is either an interesting piece of antiquity, connected with the origin of Rome ("Mavortis in antro"), or else, as in xii. 187, simply war and battle: "Sin nostrum adnuerit nobis Victoria Martem." This last is an interesting passage, as it happens, for the deity here is Victoria, now beginning the great career she had under the Empire, while the old god, the *numen* of the year, the spring, and the war-season, seems here as dead as a door-nail. Another cause of the degradation of this fine old god was the myth-making art, which could not leave him alone in this age. Ovid has shown us that; and all the shreds of legend may be found collected by Usener, in a famous paper now reprinted in the fourth volume of his *Kleine Schriften*.[1] Augustus tried to start him on a new career as *Mars Ultor*, whose temple in the Forum Augusti can still in part be traced. But Augustus, shrewd as he was, did not realise that the brief age of polytheism was over for Rome and Italy; and that by adding a cult-title after the old Roman fashion, you could not put new life into a dying deity. Once fall into the habit of using his name in vain—in

[1] Page 122 foll.

this case for the thing over which he was once believed to preside—and there is an end of him as an effective god. If von Domaszewski is right,[1] he was of no great mark even in the army until the third century, when the new military organisation placed him once more in an important official position.

Passing over the very obvious example which Venus supplies,[2] I will just take a negative instance by way of proving the rule. It is an interesting fact that the oldest Roman deity, who represents the family life on which the Roman state was built, never, so far as I can discover, had her name taken in vain as a mere synonym by her own people; that was reserved for us to do in an age of lucifer matches. Myth-making tried to lay hold on her, but without any real success; there was a peculiar *sanctitas* about her which discouraged it. "Nihil apud Romanos templo Vestae sanctius habebatur," said Augustine.[3] Vesta may be occasionally used for the domestic hearth, but such a use was not familiar to the Roman, nor is it familiar to us. The true feeling about her, surely a religious feeling even in the Augustan age, was expressed as usual by Virgil better than by any

---

[1] *Religion des röm. Heeres*, p. 34.
[2] Neptunus is of course another example, *e.g.* Hor. *Epode*, vii. 3:
  Parumne campis atque Neptuno super
  Fusum est Latini sanguinis?
This is parallel to the use of Jupiter for the heaven, which we must not forget, though it has more meaning than the other examples, as being the one which suggests the great Stoic principle of cosmic unity.
[3] *Civ. Dei*, iii. 28.

other, in the splendid passage of prophecy in the first book of the *Aeneid*:

> Aspera tum positis mitescunt saecula bellis:
> Cana Fides et Vesta, Remo cum fratre Quirinus
> Iura dabunt.

What Virgil here means by Vesta is more easily felt than explained. Servius strikingly explains her as *Religio*, but adds, alas, his reason—that no sacrifice can be without fire. But *religio* will do well enough for us, if we understand by the word both the feeling of awe that prompted to religious usage, and also the ritual itself. It is the clean pure worship of an idea which the ages have been unable to corrupt or degrade; the morality of family life enlarged into the morality of state-life. As I have said elsewhere, the simple duties of the vestal virgins preserved this beautiful cult at all times from contamination. " Far more than any other cult, that of Vesta represents the reality and continuity of Roman religious feeling." [1]

Vesta's survival could do no harm, even to Christianity. As to Apollo and the rest, their slow decay was no loss to the world; even Jupiter, as a name for something far greater than a common god, was as well out of the way. The last work of these Olympians was to give a certain distinction to Latin poetry and Roman history; then the world needed them no more.

[1] *Religious Experience*, etc., p. 137.

I will finish this lecture by a few notes on the attitude of the leading Augustan writers to religion and the gods.

Of Virgil I have already said something, *i.e.* of his share in taking the life out of Jupiter, Mars, and Apollo. But we may at least be sure that he never makes his gods ridiculous, not even his Olympians or machinery gods. Divinity was for him far too serious a matter to be taken light-heartedly, as Ovid and Propertius took it. For him, even at the outset of his poetical career, "Iovis omnia plena" (*Ecl.* iii. 60), words which show that he was already acquainted with the larger theology of his age. Virgil was of course at heart a philosopher-poet, and what he really believes in is a principle of divinity in the universe, God manifesting himself in many ways. His Olympians, if we apply this test to them, were hardly gods in Virgil's conception—they were useful helps in telling a story, but they were not the manifestation of any divine principle. But he could still persuade himself that in the *di agrestes*, in Tellus, Silvanus, the Fauni, the Manes, the Genii of men and places, there was a real manifestation of divinity, and this is why he dwells on all such *numina* with peculiar tenderness and delicacy. This, too, is why he loves the details of their cult, which is in the main with him the real old Italian worship, not a Graecised form of it. He is not *patronising* this simple worship, but feeling the beauty and the reality of it; not too definitely, not by way of dragging *numina* and worship into the glaring light of reason, but throwing a soft veil of *religio* over it all.

The religious ideas of Livy were, I think, much the same as Virgil's. Both came from the same district, perhaps of the same stock. His humanity and his instinct for righteousness make it difficult to see what he really thinks about the gods and the worship of his day; but he never sneers at either, handling them always tenderly. He has Virgil's feeling for religious antiquities, and the same instinct for avoiding too great definiteness about them. " Detur haec venia antiquitati, ut miscendo humana divinis, primordia urbium augustiora faciat " (*Praefatio*). He has no sympathy with the myth-making faculty as it affects divinity, and did nothing, any more than Virgil, to bring into contempt the idea of the divine.

The same may be said of Tibullus; compared with Ovid or Propertius, he has little room for the Alexandrian mythology, though a few allusions to myths will be found scattered about in his poems.[1] In the third elegy of Bk. i. he shows a leaning towards the religion of Isis—but then Delia was a devotee. Bellona-Ma and Osiris claimed him, but he seems to wish to hold by his own gods after all: " At mihi contingat patrios celebrare Penates " (33 foll.). He never deserted them, never even doubted them, I think; his is the simplest conservative religious creed of the Augustan age. The details of rural

---

[1] *E.g.* i. 3. 67 foll.

worship are his especial delight; and if we may judge of the genuineness of a poet's feeling by the beauty of his workmanship, as I think we often may, Tibullus may be taken as a real believer in the *di agrestes*. He has known them all his life and he cannot abandon them. When he expects to be sent on military service he hopes that his *Lares* will watch over him, in language that seems to me unmistakably to ring true: [1]

> Sed patrii servate Lares; aluistis et idem
> Cursarem vestros cum tener ante pedes.

Read this charming poem, and also the first and second of Book ii., in order to realise that if the Olympians were dying, the rural divinities meant something still for gentle minds. It is remarkable that even in his long national or semi-official poem (ii. 5), he reverts at the end to the old shepherds' festival of the Palilia, treating it in his simple genuine way.

Horace's poems, if taken in chronological order (so far as we can be sure about it), form an interesting study of a gifted man's religious ideas. Professor Granger not long ago pointed out in the *Classical Review* (March 1910) that Horace did not always see the divine in the same light; and this is sufficiently obvious to any one who reads through his works with religion in his mind. We know that the *Epodes* and the *Satires* come first in chronological order; and

[1] i. 10. 15.

they tell us very little, unless it be that Horace was not interested in these things. At the same time there is hardly any mythology, and no trace of a leaning towards oriental cults, such as we saw in Tibullus. You will remember that at the end of the journey to Brundisium Horace declines to believe in an apparent miracle—

> Credat Iudaeus Apella,
> Non ego;

for his faith is that of Epicurus, that gods do not trouble themselves about the wonders of nature. In *Sat.* i. 8 there is a mocking tone, which reminds us of Ovid:

> Olim truncus eram ficulnus, inutile lignum,
> um faber, incertus scamnum faceretne Priapum,
> Maluit esse deum. Deus inde ego, furum aviumque
> Maxima formido.

In *Sat.* i. 6. 114 we find him looking in at some "evening service" (*adsisto divinis*), while he saunters about the Circus and Forum. I imagine that this was not actual sacrifice, but the later process after the *exta* had been placed on the altar; and it was then, I think, that the prayer was uttered.[1] Like Ovid, when he saw the priests making for the grove of Robigus with the *exta* of a dog,[2] Horace "adsistit" perhaps mainly out of curiosity, and like Ovid, notes the nature of the prayer, with complete aloofness, neither mocking nor sympathising. Such at least is my idea of him on the whole, as he shows himself in

---

[1] *Religious Experience*, p. 181.   [2] *Fasti*, iv. 905 foll.

these early poems, "parcus deorum cultor et infrequens," like any one else in society.

When we come to the next period of Horace's artistic life, that of the first three books of the *Odes* and the establishment of Augustus's power, the contrast to all this is striking—enough by itself, I think, to separate the periods pretty clearly as regards literary work. All through these odes the gods abound; you would imagine the poet's mind teeming with religious and mythological associations. All I can do here is to point out how far this bears on the subject of this lecture.

First, let us notice that the Stoic idea of deity shows itself here and there: it is in fact the educated man's belief, whether reasoned out or no. We see it in the use of *deus* for the divine principle in the world, as in i. 3. 21.[1] Another passage[2] has some interest, for the context shows that *fortuna* means much the same thing—the power over our lives for which we cannot account, as I explained in my third lecture:

> Valet ima summis
> Mutare et insignem attenuat *deus*,
> Obscura promens: hinc apicem rapax
> Fortuna cum stridore acuto
> Sustulit, hic posuisse gaudet.

Wickham does not agree that *fortuna* and *deus* are here co-ordinated; but his distinction between them is too subtle. Is not Horace thinking in this

---

[1] Cp. i. 18. 3 and 34. 13, iii. 16 *ad fin.*   [2] i. 34. 13.

ode, *Parcus deorum,* of the grip Lucretius once had on him, with whom, as we have seen, *fortuna* is very near to *natura rerum* ? This ode is worth close attention, for it does not seem quite in earnest, and yet it probably expresses Horace's sense of finding an opportunity to fall into line with the Augustan revival of religion.

Secondly, gods of all kinds and in all aspects are to be found in this first book. Faunus of the villa (i. 17) puts him in a mood of rural *pietas* that is not quite natural to him but delightful to us:

> Di me tuentur, dis pietas mea
> Et musa cordi est.[1]

Mercurius-Hermes he treats (10) with charming jocoseness, handling the mischievous boy with comic tenderness. The Olympians are here too, in court dress: Apollo and Diana in 21, and in 31 the Apollo of the new temple on the Palatine. Once or twice Augustus himself is touched in, though with the caution needed in so delicate a matter. On the whole Books i. and ii. illustrate the inevitable tendency of the poets of this age to make much play with gods as well as men, for the gods are their poetical inheritance. In ii. 1, for example, we think we are going to get off with Fortuna in the first stanza, but no—" Iuno et deorum quisquis amicior " seems to lend a certain distinction to the poem ; and so beyond doubt the Roman reader fancied. In the individualistic or human odes that

---

[1] Cp. iii. 13 and 18.

follow this one we do not find them; but in 7 and 10 they intrude themselves again. In 19 Dionysus is the subject of the whole ode.

The first six earnest odes of Bk. iii., about which so much has been written, only help us in this way—that in spite of their appeal to righteousness, there is little trace of an appeal to religion in its support. The sixth is the only one of which this can be said; the performance of the outward forms of religion is declared to be the necessary preliminary of moral progress. Apart from that ode, I find nothing except the warning at the end of the second to keep good faith—for

> Saepe Diespiter
> Neglectus incesto addidit integrum.

There is abundance of mythical allusion; in the third the machinery reminds us of the *Aeneid*, and the effect is undoubtedly fine. The Caesar-cult crops up two or three times, and is treated with dignity if we except the

> Augustus recumbens
> Purpureo bibet ore nectar.[1]

That Augustus really wished his poets to emphasise the connexion between religion and ethics, between the old Roman morals and the old Roman worship, there can be no doubt; but in these odes, all but the sixth, the lesson is not enforced. In the fourth book and the *Carmen saeculare* it is much more

---

[1] iii. 3. 11. Here *bibet* should certainly be the right reading, and was adopted by Wickham in the Oxford text of 1904. See above, p. 128.

obvious. In the *Carmen*, as I have pointed out elsewhere, it has been worked in with such pains as to lose all real poetical effect.

Roughly we may say that as the Horatian quietism and indifference gradually become disturbed by the political necessities of Augustus, the poet develops a kind of quasi-religious feeling in three ways : (1) he occasionally represents cosmic forces under the name either of *deus* simply, or of Jupiter or some other mythological figure ; (2) he enjoys doing his own little acts of simple cult at his farm in the Sabine hills ; (3) he yields to the popular view of Augustus as Sôter and Euergetes, and as thus ready for deification, if not already on the full footing of a god.

Of all the poets the one most destitute of religion is Propertius. I can find in him no sense of God, either as cosmic ruler, or genial *deus agrestis* in the old Italian sense. In the three first books I will note one passage only, which shows what the gods were coming to, and that it was high time to have done with them. Cynthia has made the goddesses jealous, and now she is ill in the feverish season.

> Sed non tam ardoris culpa est neque crimina caeli,
>   quam totiens sanctos non habuisse deos.
> Hoc perdit miseras, hoc perdidit ante puellas :
>   quidquid iurarunt, ventus et unda rapit.

A girl breaks her promise to her lover—this is where Propertius's art finds godliness useful ! So too at the end of the poem.[1]

---
[1] Propertius ii. 28 *passim*.

In Bk. iv. there is plenty of magic and mythology—all quite cold, but very often pretty enough. There is a domestic passage in the first elegy of this book, where he had a good chance to show some tenderness for the gods of the family; but he lets it slip by with the merest allusion. The second elegy, the well-known one about Vertumnus, is charming in its way, and reminds us of the *Fasti* of Ovid, where the gods are merely a part of the artistic material with which a skilful designer is working.

The cult of Augustus seems to appeal to Propertius in some degree, and in iv. 6. 36 Augustus is hailed as " mundi servator," Sôter that is, as in the Greek inscriptions of the period. This elegy, which is almost genuine in feeling, celebrates the foundation of Apollo's temple on the Palatine, and the poets could usually do better with Apollo than with the rest. But even this is full of frozen mythology. It is all cool even to iciness.

Though Propertius seems to me to be the chilliest of the Augustan poets in regard to religion, it is with Ovid that we reach the lowest depths of degradation. Ovid's poetry is so voluminous that it would be wearisome to cull examples from all his works; nor are they equally important in this respect. Let us take mainly the *Fasti* and the *Metamorphoses*. The chief distinction between these two is that the subject of the *Fasti* is Roman, and therefore has to do largely with the cult, being thus incidentally valuable; while the *Metamorphoses* are almost pure Greek in origin—

Greek of the Hellenistic age—and therefore consist almost wholly of myth.

Even in the *Fasti* there is no real religious feeling: unlike Virgil, Ovid is entirely outside his subject, stands quite aloof from it. He has the spirit of curiosity and the skill of a consummate artist, but not a spark of genuine feeling. He does not mock at the details of the cult, for that would not have suited Augustus; but he admits some quaint scenes, and evidently enjoys describing them. The humour of the poem is indeed one of its most interesting features. We see it in the way in which he treats some of the gods; to Greek fancy is added a kind of comical Romanism, as in the stories of Janus and Mars, or rather in the interview with the one and the myths about the other. The whole material, as Schanz says of the myths,[1] is simply matter for his artistic skill. His desire to interest the reader is much the strongest motive, and the method of treatment is really useful in indicating the taste of the time at Rome.

Only when he comes to the cult of Vesta in June[2] does the whole tone seem to rise a little. Vesta, as we have seen, was an unsoiled and genuine religious conception, and was too near to the idea of Dea Roma, now beginning to be associated with Augustus, to be handled wantonly. He says that he used to think there was a statue of Vesta in her temple. He found out that he was wrong:

[1] *Gesch. der röm. Literatur*, Pt. II. i. 312. [2] *Fasti*, vi. 290 foll.

Ignis inextinctus templo celatur in illo.
Effigiem nullam Vesta nec ignis habet.

Here was an opportunity for a little mysticism, or at least reverence, if he had been disposed for it; but he knew the taste of his readers, and strays away into a "multi fabula parva ioci." The religious conception is for him no longer unsoiled.

There is one passage of real feeling in Ovid about the gods. It is at the beginning of the *Tristia*, where he bids farewell to the city on his way to exile. The beauty of the Ovidian art is here at last combined with real feeling—I remember well how deeply it affected me at a very tender age—for the divine as well as the human inhabitants of the city:

> Numina vicinis habitantia sedibus, inquam,
>   Iamque oculis nunquam templa videnda meis,
> Dique relinquendi, quos urbs tenet alta Quirini,
>   Este salutati tempus in omne mihi.[1]

Yet almost directly afterwards these gods were prayed to intercede with Augustus ("caelestis vir")—and after all, the lines now leave an odd taste in my mouth.

In the *Metamorphoses* Ovid uses what we may call a legitimate material for his skill and his fancy, playing lightly over the whole range of Hellenic and Hellenistic myth, and happily destroying for ever all chance of a resuscitation of polytheism among the educated classes in the empire.[2] It is this work,

---

[1] *Tristia*, i. 3. 33 foll.

[2] It is of course the same in Alexandrian or Hellenistic art. Professor E. Gardner expresses this briefly but to the point (*Religion and Art in*

always so popular in the Middle Ages, that more than any other has prevented us moderns from finding anything but pure nonsense in that system of polytheism. But it is not here that we learn what Ovid really thought about the gods, it is in that far more questionable work, the *Ars Amoris*, throughout which he speaks his own mind freely. In Bk. i. 631 foll. he advises the youth to learn how to deceive his girl with impunity ("fallite fallentes," 645) : you may safely break your promise, he says, for Jupiter used to do the very same thing, swearing falsely by the Styx to Juno. Then he goes on—

> Expedit esse deos, et, ut expedit, esse putemus :
> Dentur in antiquos tura merumque focos :

it is good for us that there should be gods, and that being so, let us suppose they really exist, let us carry on their old cults conscientiously.

> Nec secura quies illos similisque sopori
> Detinet : innocue vivite, numen adest.
> Reddite depositum, pietas sua foedera servet :
> Fraus absit, vacuas caedis habete manus :
> Ludite, si sapitis, solas impune puellas.[1]

I paraphrase again : " If we can fancy there are gods, let us at least believe them active and awake, not

---

Ancient Greece, p. 116). Speaking of the famous Nile statue he says : " It is not like the earlier gods, who were looked on as the givers of increase and fertility : it is a mere allegorical impersonation of the river, such as might be made by a modern artist. . . . It cannot be counted as religious art at all. And the attributes and accessories of such a figure . . . are all of them symbolic allusions suitable to such a frigid personification."

[1] Brandt's note on this passage shows that this maxim was of very old standing in Greek literature. It is found also in Tibullus, i. 4. 21.

like those of Epicurus with their quietism and their slumber. No, let us keep faith and do right, imagining that they are not far from us; but if you make an exception and break faith with your girl, remember that they won't mind that!" I do not know that the popular attitude towards the gods and their worship was ever so well expressed. Does any one but a fanatic really believe in them? No. Does any one but a fanatic really propose to do without them? Again the answer is No. "Nothing shows us more clearly," says Wilamowitz (*Apollo*, p. 44), "how dead the gods really were, than the writers who are trying earnestly to believe in them." Yet still stronger, surely, is the evidence of those who make them into literary playthings, or at the best, artistic ornaments.

It is impossible to recover the religious psychology of that age; no excavations can reveal it, as they have revealed so many things that were unknown before. But it is possible that these few lectures may have suggested some points of interest likely to lead us a little nearer to the understanding we wish for, though without any attempt at a symmetrical survey. I asked myself what the old Roman religion could contribute to the idea of deity, and found some little contribution in the spirituality of the domestic worships, especially of Genius, and in the tendency towards monotheism in the cult of Jupiter the heaven-god. I went on to remark on the sense of cosmic

THE AUGUSTAN AGE

powers as divine forces—the sun and the beginnings of astrology, and Fortuna in the varying senses of deity, nature (the natural order of things), or simply blind chance. Then I passed to the most important of the religious tendencies of the age, the tendency to think of Man as capable of becoming god, and the exemplification of this tendency in the cult of the Caesars, which re-constituted the old connexion between religion and the State. Lastly, I have traced in literature the degradation of the old polytheism through the killing off of the most eminent Graeco-Roman deities by conventional and symbolic use of their names.

What have we learnt from all this discussion? Our results seem at first sight to be meagre enough; and in a theological sense, that is no doubt true. But if we allow ourselves a slightly wider outlook, we may possibly find that something was gained for humanity by the Italian way of looking at the divine, even in that depressing age, the last century B.C.; something solid and practical, as compared with the ever-shifting kaleidoscope of fanciful speculation and allegory which survives to bewilder us in the Graeco-Egyptian literature of this and the following age.

First, the evergreen idea of guardian deities of the family, especially in the rural districts of Italy, kept alive the sense of a close relation of Man and God at the very roots of social life, day by day, through good fortune and ill. In the idea of Genius, too, we see another point of close contact between the human and the divine, again in association with the ordering of society and the rule of the family; no doubt losing some of its old strength and meaning in this age, yet extending itself to inspire many institutions of society and government with a kind of spiritual vigour not without its real value. Then again we have seen how the Power manifesting itself in the universe, and manifesting itself at that time more especially in the wonders of the Roman dominion, could be represented under the name of Jupiter, who seemed to gather the various old *numina* syncretically into a deity like that of the Stoics, a deity of Law and Order, one divine Being, whatever his name might be — a more valuable conception, perhaps, for humanity in the long run than the wilder individualistic worships of Cybele, Isis, or Mithras.

Once more, the worship of the Man in power, so extravagant in the eastern half of the empire and beyond it, was kept in bounds in Italy and Rome by the practical and non-theological character of the native religious ideas. It was taken in hand by the government, restricted as far as possible to the cult of the Man who *had been* in power, and might be supposed at death to have merely developed the germ of divinity—the Genius—which was all along within him when he lived. Passionate worship of the living man, *devotio*, for example, to the *numen* of the reigning Caesar, is the exception, not the rule.

Lastly, the final degradation in this age of the pseudo-Olympian deities, as we may now call them, was surely a great gain for humanity, since they had now entirely lost such inspiration as they once possessed. No longer really respected, they found a refuge in literature, and made room in the world of life and thought for new and nobler ideas. True, the student of the *Corpus*, or even of the *Carmina Epigraphica*, might argue that they survived, especially in the Latin provinces, throughout the first three centuries of the empire; their names are on altars and *ex-votos* wherever we look for them. But the most careful investigators [1] have noticed that in the strings of divine names which puzzle the student all over the western provinces, we are to see a tendency at once syncretistic and monotheistic, the old tendency to focus the manifestations of the Power at one point, and so to bring all its force to bear on the matter of interest to the worshipper. This is, however, a subject needing further investigation. Let me conclude by suggesting it to some of my hearers as one of real value, in more ways than one, for the student of the life and thought of the imperial period.

[1] The subject is reasonably discussed by M. Toutain (*Cultes païens*, ii. 227 foll.). He endorses the results arrived at long ago by Jean Réville and accepted by Wissowa and others. See also Dill, *Roman Society in Last Century of Western Empire*, 77 foll. J. B. Carter, *Religious Life in Ancient Rome*, p. 45, maintains, however, that in Julian's time the old gods were still living realities.

INDEX

Academica (Cicero's), 4
Adorable, the (Bhagavat), 34
Adsisto divinis, 149
Aesculapius, 139
Agahd, 82
Agesilaus, 99
Agrippa, 16; as a priest, 124
Alba Longa, 95.
Alexander, 96, 99, 101
Ancestors, cult of, 35
Anchises, 24
Anima mundi, 82
Animism, traditional, and divinity, 12; Vesta and Penates, survivals of, 15, 16
Antiochus, 6
Antony, 112, 120, 122
Aphrodite, 114
Apollo, 61, 139, 141, 145, 146, 151; of Augustus, 60; a god of healing, 138; a god of music and poetry, 138; temple on the Palatine, 140; under the name Phoibos, 141; a god of medicine, 142
Apotheosis, 98
Apuleius, 80; quoted, 19
Ara Pacis, 138
Ares, 114
Aristotle, 69, 89, 91
Arnim, von, 50
Arnold, Mr. E. V., 50, 53
Athena, 130
Augustus, 58, 95, 98, 104, 126, 129, 155; deification of, 88; divinity of, 123; as *euergetes*, 124; as *pater patriae*, 124; as Pontifex Maximus, 124; as a priest, 124; as saviour, 124; as *praesens deus*, 127; as *vir maxime*, 127; built a temple to Apollo on the Palatine, 137; Prima Porta statue of, 138; his attitude to religion and the gods, 154; as "mundi servator," 154
Aulus Gellius, 68

Bellona-Ma, 147
Bevan, Mr. E. R., 111
Boissier, 104
Brasidas, 99
Buecheler, 79

Caecus, Appius Claudius, 65
Caeleste numen, 77
Caelestes, dei, 93
Caesar, Julius, 42, 43, 75, 98, 105, 117, 121; cult of, 112; deified as Sôter and Euergetes, 114; his statue inscribed Deo Invicto, 115, 116
Caesar-worship, 13, 88, 108, 132
Caird, Dr., quoted, 6; his *Evolution of Religion in the Greek Philosophies* referred to, 7, 50
Carlyle, 91
Cattle, white, as an offering, 38
Catullus, 139
Charles, Dr., 23
Cicero, 2, 3, 4, 7, 10, 25, 30, 46-49, 81-87, 90, 95, 101, 105, 139; a Roman man of the world, 5; his theology, 8; his view of *superstitio*, 8; Dr. Mayor on, 8; the real value of his work, 10; quoted, 41; what he thought of the Stoic deity, 50 *et seq.*; his idea of Fortuna, 71 *et seq.*
Cleanthes, 51

ROMAN IDEAS OF DEITY

Conway, Professor, 105
Corn-doles, 110
Cornelius Nepos, 76, 112
Cult of the dead, 22
Cult-titles of Jupiter, 43, 45
Cumont, M., 2, 50, 56, 58, 59, 90, 121, 141
Curio, 42, 43
Cybele, 160
Cynthia, 153

d' Alviella, Count Goblet, 35
δαίμων, 90
Dea Roma, 155; Caesar-worship and, 131 *et seq.*
Dei, 23
Deities, household (*familia*), 14; men of talent recognised as, 13; Roman, forces of nature, 92
Delia, 147
Demetrius, 99
Deorum, de Natura (Cicero's), its value and shortcomings, 2 *et seq.*; referred to, 50 *et seq.*
Deus, 16, 17, 18, 19, 70, 89, 105, 129, 150, 153
Di, 22, 23, 24; protecting spirits of the family, 23
Di agrestes, 146, 148
Di aquatiles, 16
Di coniugales, 16
Di inferi, 16
Di Manes, 16, 19, 23
Di parentum, 16, 22, 23
Di Penates, 15, 16, 17, 23
Diana, 151
Dio Cassius, 115
Diodorus Siculus, 99
Dionysus, 152
Dius Fidius, 41
Divinatione, de (Cicero's), 4, 8, 9
Divinum numen, 45
Divinus, 89
Divus, 129
Divus Iulius, 123; one of the gods of the State, 122
Dolabella, 120
Domaszewski, von, 118, 119, 133, 144
Dux et princeps, sun as, 59

Empedocles, 47; claimed to be a god, 88

Emperor, worship of the, 88
Ennius, 101, 102
Epicureans, 26, 84
Epicurus, 47, 88, 100, 137
Euergetes, 112, 118
Euhemerus, 100, 101
Eutropius, 113
Exta, 149

False swearer, 42, 43
Familia, 14
Family, worship of the, 12
Farnell, Dr., 56
Fate, 81; the product of the brain of philosophers, in Cicero, 73
Fato, de (Cicero's), 4
Fatum, 73; *bonum*, 17 *n.*
Fauni, 146
Faunus, 93, 94, 151
Feriae Latinae, 38
Festivals of Jupiter, 38, 44
Fetials, 39, 40
Fides, 41
Finibus, de (Cicero's), 4, 19
Flamen, 118, 122
Flamen Dialis, 39, 97
Flamininus, 99, 110
Flaminium Diale, 119 *n.*
Fors, 62, 63
Fors Fortuna, 64
Fortuna, 13, 49, 61, 62, 68, 70, 73-75, 79, 81, 133, 134, 150, 151, 159; a power in human life, 61; a Latin deity, 62; concerned with foretelling the future, 63; her cult-title, 63; Jupiter's first-born, 63; a woman's deity, 64, 65; temples in Rome, 65; publica Populi Romani, 65, 78; as a wanton power, 76, 77; *dea*, 79
Fortuna-Isis, 78
Fortuna and Jupiter, 45
Fortuna Redux, 17 *n.*
Fortune, 69
Frank, Professor Tenney, 40
Frazer, Dr. J. G., 92, 96, 97

Galen, 89
Gardner, Professor E., quoted, 156 *n.*
Gardner, Professor P., 91, 136
Genii, 146
Genius, 17-22, 27, 90, 91, 106, 123, 132, 133, 158-160; *loci*, 17 *n.*; of

INDEX

the paterfamilias, 17; wine an offering to, 18; described in Horace, 18; the divine force of life and action, 20; applied to the old gods, 20; Iovis, 20; Cicero and, 21; ascribed to institutions, 21; under the Empire, 21; the permanent principle in social life, 22; worship in the household, 27; expressed the power of the head of the family to carry on its life within the *gens*, 28
Genius venalicius, 21
Γένος, 94
Gens, 17, 22, 28, 94; Julia, 113
Gentes, religion of, 95
Gods, the divine inhabitants of the City-state, 84
Granger, Professor, 148
Greenidge, Dr., 94
Grierson, Dr., 33

Heaven-god, 40, 43; as the Power sanctioning oath, 42
Heifer, white, as an offering, 38
Heinze, on Fortuna in Virgil, 77
Hekataeus, 99, 100
Hera, 99
Hercules, a god, 93
Horace, 11; quoted, 18, 127; his attitude to religion and the gods, 148 *et seq.*
Hose and McDougall's *Pagan Tribes of Borneo*, quoted, 32; referred to, 55

Ides, 44
Immortalis, 19
Indiges, cult-title, 57
Individualism, 102
Invocatio, in Lucretius, 48
Iovem lapidem, 39
Isis, 80, 86, 100, 147, 160; as Fortuna, 80
Ius divinum, 117
Iustum, 40

Jahveh, 36
Janus, 29, 155
Jordan, H., 45
Julii, 95, 114
Juno, 29, 157
Jupiter 30, 34, 40-46, 55-97, 105, 119, 145, 146, 158, 160; the Father of Heaven, 37; the Latin, 37; what he was to the Latin tribes, 37; cult-titles, 43, 45; of the Capitol, 43, 52-54; of the Alban hill, 44; a supreme deity, 44; ides great festivals of, 44; and Juno, 44; as king of gods and men, 51; Capitol dedicated to, 52; as a creative intelligence, 52

King, divinity of, 96
King, inscriptions in honour of, 100
Kings, worship of, 92

Lake, Professor, on "God-fearers," 5; his *Earlier Epistles of St. Paul* referred to, 5
Lang, Andrew, on a supreme deity among primitive peoples, 34
Lares, 148; *compitales*, 124
Lebensgeist, 133
Leo, Egyptian priest, 99
Livy, 40, 43, 76, 77, 112; his attitude to religion and the gods, 147
Love, the mistress of *Rerum natura*, 48
Lucius, in Apuleius, 80
Lucretius, 3, 8-10, 26, 30, 46, 48, 49, 74, 88, 139
Ludi circenses, 115; *Romani*, 117; *saeculares*, 124, 129, 140
Luperci Iuliani, 118
Lyall, Sir A., 94
Lysander, 99

Macella, 21
Magistrate, oath taken by, 40
Man, as "deus mortalis," 19; subject to the "economy of nature," 70; worship of, 86; divine element in, 90; Roman repugnance to the worship of, 99
Man-god, 106, 134; in Greece, 98; in Egypt, 99
Manes, 146
Mannhardt, 57
Marius Gratidianus, 111
Mars, 29, 30, 114, 143, 146, 155
Mars Ultor, his temple in the Forum Augusti, 143
Mayor, Dr. Joseph B., 1, 9, 10; quoted, 8; on Cicero, 8

Meal, sacramental, 37, 38
Mediusfidius, 41
Mehercule, 41
Memmii, 114
Metellus Pius, 111
Milk offerings, 38
Mithras, 60, 160
Monotheism, first stage traceable in theology, 35
Moon, chief deity in Babylonia, 55
Murray, Professor G., 80 *n.*, 135
Mystery religions, 14, 103

Natura, 49, 73, 74; *rerum*, 151
Nemesis, 64, 69
Neptunus, 30
Nettleship, H., 93
Norden, 2
Numen, 11, 12, 15, 16, 24, 30, 37, 39, 45, 48, 53-55, 62, 101, 130-133, 135, 143, 146, 160
Numen Augusti, 132, 133

Oath, Fetial, 40; by the Heaven-god, 39, 40; taken in the open, 41; power of, at Rome, 41, 42; civilising power of, 43
Obelisks dedicated to the sun-god, 60
Offering, given to Fortuna by women, 63
Officiis, de (Cicero's), 4, 7
Oracles, 62
Orosius, 113
Osiris, 100, 147
Otto, W., 132
Ovid, 30, 114, 143, 154

Pacuvius, 62
Palilia, 148
Panaetius, 51, 59, 67, 68, 72, 89
Panthea, 78
Parentalia, 24
Pelham, Professor, 125, 126
Penates, 27, 40; worship in the household, 27; expressed the continuity of the household's means of subsistence, 28
Periurium, 43
Petrie, Professor W. M. Flinders, 35
Pettazzoni, Dr., 35, 36
Phaethon, 136
Philodemus, 6
Phoebus, 139, 140, 142

Pietas, 141
Πίστις, 130
Plato, 12; called a god, 89
Plautus, 66
Pliny, 79, 121
Plutarch, 41, 142
Polybius, 42, 52, 67, 68, 96; quoted, 71
Posidonius, 6, 12, 54, 58, 59, 90, 142; Syrian, 2; what he thought of the Stoic deity, 50 *et seq.*
Praeneste, 45
Preller, 57
Priest, of Jupiter, 39
Primigenia, Fortuna's cult-title, 63
Princeps, 125
Propertius, 30; his attitude to religion and the gods, 153
Ptolemy I., 100

Quintilian, 137
Quirinus, 30, 93

Reid, Professor J. S., 6, 7
Religio, 8, 17, 42, 86, 145, 147
Religion, of the family, 14; of astrology, 121
Republica, de (Cicero's), 4
Rerum natura, 47; Love, the mistress of, 48
Roma, cult of, 130
Roma aeterna, 17 *n.*
Roman, the, and the Heaven-god, 42
Roman deities, functional forces of nature, 92
Roman idea of worship of the family, 12; worship of the State, 12
Romans, their conception of divinity, 11; men of talent recognised as deities, 13; good faith among, 41
Romulus, 114, 116
Ross, Mr., Scottish missionary, quoted, 31
Rulers, worship of, 88, 103

Sacrifice, head of the State offered, 38
St. Augustine, 52, 82, 99; quoted, 20
Sallust, 76, 111, 112
Sanctitas, 144
Sanctus, 139
Sardus Pater, 36

INDEX   167

Saussaye, Chantepie de la, 31
Scaevola, 89
Scipio Aemilianus, 68
Scipio Africanus, 43, 110
Seneca, 7
Servius, 61, 145
Silex, 40
Silvanus, 93, 146 ; a real god, 94
Sky-god, 41
Smith, Robertson, 38
Sol, 56, 57
Sol Indiges, 57, 60
Sol Invictus, creator and saviour of man, 59
Somnium Scipionis (Cicero's), 4, 59
Sophocles, 89
Soracte, 57
Soranus, 56 ; taken for the sun by Preller and Mannhardt, 57
Sors, 79
Sortes, 63
Sôter, 110, 112
Soul, a divine thing, 90
Soul of the world, sun as, 59 : doctrine of, 81
State, worship of the, 12
Stoics and Jupiter, 50 *et seq.*
Strabo, 2
Suetonius, 107
Sulla, 111
Sun, 55, 58, 81, 85 ; the god of kings, 58 ; ruler of the heavens, 59 ; an intelligent power, 59
Sun-god, obelisks to, 60
Sun-worship, 33, 55, 141, 142 ; work of astronomers, 56
Superstitio, 8, 9, 86

Taboos of Flamen Dialis, 39
Tacitus, 87, 88
Tatius, 57
Tellus, 146
Terence, 66
Terentia, 139
Theocritus, 140
Θεός, 70
Tiberius, 131
Tibullus, his attitude to religion and the gods, 147

Toutain, M., 53, 132, 142
Τύχη, 61, 66, 68 ; a power influencing men's lives, 69 ; a cosmic power or process, 69 *et seq.*
Tullia, 4
Tusculans (Cicero's), 4, 7
Tutela, 133
Twin Brethren, as gods, 93
Tylor, 94

Universal Reason, doctrine of, 81
Usener, 143

Valerius Maximus, 113
Varro, 3, 21, 22, 46, 57-59, 81 *et seq.*, 94, 105
Veddahs of Ceylon, 93
Veiovis, 95
Velleius, 88, 113
Venerandus, 139
Venus, 49, 95, 144 ; reputed ancestor of the Romans, 48
Venus Erycina, 95
Venus Genetrix, 48, 114
Venus Victrix, 113
Vesta, 15, 16, 27, 144, 145, 155 ; symbolised the continuity of the family life, 27 ; worship in the household, 27
Victoria, 143
Virgil, 8, 48, 60, 76, 104, 126, 144 ; his attitude to religion and the gods, 146
Virgin Mary, 27
Virtus, 66, 133
Vishnu, cult of, a form of sun-worship, 33

Wendland, 2, 100
Westermarck, 41, 43
Wilamowitz, quoted, 158
Wine, libation to Genius, 18
Wissowa, quoted, 16 ; referred to, 44
World-soul, 81, 85, 86, 105
Worship, of the family, 12 ; of the State, 12

Zeus, 51, 59, 99, 100
Zeus of Olympia, 137
Zielinski referred to, 7

www.ingramcontent.com/pod-product-compliance
Lightning Source LLC
Chambersburg PA
CBHW051102160426
43193CB00010B/1281